TRIAL AND ERROR

LIFE OF DEPRESSION

ROBERT L. LAWSON

Book Layout © 2022 Robert Lawson

Printed in the USA:

Trial and Error, Life of Depression
Robert L. Lawson-1st Ed. ISBN: (979-8-218-13887-5)

Library of Congress Control Number:(2023900991)

DEDICATION

I dedicate this book to my grandmother Karin Taylor who passed on February 27, 2021. She was my everything and still is. She was always encouraging me to do the right things in life and if it wasn't for what she said a couple weeks before she passed, I would've never known my purpose in life. So, thank you granny for everything. I love you so much and I will continue to carry on your name and continue to do the right things in life, like you always wanted me to do.

NOTES TO READER

This book talks about the impressions and ideas of the writer and the intention are to provide awareness into what the author has learned over his years of growing up. The author does not give medical information or says its right to use any of the methods in the book whether it be mental, physical, or spiritual...etc. The intent of the author is to give the reader information of wide-ranging value to help you along your journey. If you implement any of the references in this book, the author and publisher assume no responsibility for your actions.

ACKNOWLEDGMENTS

I want to give a very special shout out to God for never giving up on me. Thank you for allowing me and giving me the strength to tell my story. I also want to give a big shout out to my wife Danielle Lawson. You are the rock of our family. Every dream I ever wanted to accomplish; you were always right there. I mentioned I wanted to write a book and you pushed me and reminded me that I didn't have to be afraid. You encouraged me to be myself and make my own way and I thank you so much for that. I also want to acknowledge Sinatra Taylor. You held me accountable and would always ask if my book was done yet. Thank you for making sure I was staying true to my word.

ACKNOWLEDGMENTS

TABLE OF CONTENTS

YOU HAVE A HIGHER MOTIVE

Finding your motive and purpose in life can sometimes be hard and confusing. Purpose is the reason why most things in life really exist. Often times life and social media contribute to why a lot of individuals feel like they're not living out their purpose or feel as if they are not good enough. I have seen a lot of young men and young woman feel this way, including myself. I'm here to tell you that you have a lot to be proud of, and a lot to get ready for. The day you truly understand this, it'll help you create a better life and help with decision making which ultimately leads to better life choices. The very first step is to find out why you are on this earth. This is something only you can do. Nobody can do this for you, only you! Never Place limitations on your life.

1

My grandma once taught me that and she lived by this every day. She fought and fought until she had no fight left in her. The doctors tried to put limitations on her life she didn't let them she still continued to fight. It doesn't matter if you come from the ghetto, just know that will not be your final destination. It doesn't matter if you were raised by one parent, abused, molested, etc. you are still destined for greatness. All these things happen for you to make you stronger and help make your life more meaningful. My purpose for writing this book came from the pain I experienced in my childhood and the sadness I felt for not having my father around to help create the man I should've been a long time ago. There were so many times I called out for my father's love and affection but unfortunately, I was just left facing reality with a massive whole in my heart. I was torn and damaged with thoughts running through my mind such as why me?

Chapter 1

LOST AND
UNDEVELOPED CHILD

Growing up as young men and women we all imagine a life where we can become firefighters, NBA/NFL stars, doctors, nurses and so much more. Who would've thought life would often times end up being unfair, depressive, stressful, and a huge joke? We all are lost in some type of way, shape or form. When you are lost you feel hopeless. My father was in and out my life since I was 6 years old. This is the age where young Kings and Queens need that male role model in their life. Those are supposed to be the years of great learning but instead it was years of yearning for something I would never receive. I was supposed to learn how to become a man, learn who I am, how to have work ethic, build credit and many other things. However, because of the absence of my father, I became poorly developed in every aspect of my life. I was in a position to be the "man" of the house very early on which is something I had no idea how to do.

As a young man this was the time where I needed support and love, but I was alone. I was not ready to take on this responsibility without a role model. There are a lot of individuals who are just like me, undeveloped, un-coached, and unprepared because someone didn't step up and left. If this, is you, I just want you to know that life happens and you are meant to be here. It wasn't until later on in my life where I had a sit down with myself and taught myself everything that I lacked. Many of us that come from these circumstances tend to suffer the most due to lack of structure and no role models to turn to. If you were to have children or people following you, they tend to suffer too. It's an ongoing cycle. By me not having the right skills in life it had a deleterious effect on my life in so many ways. I was not ready for the real world. What made it even worse, I was following people that weren't ready either. I was yearning for love and trying to fill my void. If you are not prepared in life, how can you lead someone else?

We live in a world where men still have accessibility to make babies but are not held accountable for them. "Growing up without a father figure has a profound effect on boys that last into manhood. Boys need a father figure to learn how to be a man. Without having this influence in their lives, boys are at risk of growing into men who have problems with behavior, emotional stability, and relationships with both significant others and their own children" (Guertin, 2019). Not having the right tools and resources to become a great father, creates a norm of passing down the same behavioral patterns. Any man can create a child, but it takes a real man who's well put together and mature to raise a village. So many young adults are driven to learn the hard way in life. As a father you must instill the right mindset into your child and sow something great in them . Give them the resources so that they can one day conquer the world. We must make sure they maintain this information and know truly they are ready. If a child doesn't know they were destined for greatness, how can they ever obtain it? Without the proper guidance It can lead the child into destructive behaviors.

We have so many people misleading our children now adays such as: fake drug dealers, athletes, and music producers. We tend to teach them that's its ok to sell drugs, miss school, drop out. Our children will always be undeveloped with this mindset. Majority of these people are undeveloped, but nobody sees it because they're too busy faking lifestyles with their money, girls, and other things. We tend to always want the easy way in life. Everything that's gold isn't always good. Just because these drug dealers have a lot of money doesn't mean being a drug dealer is the right path to take. There are always consequences to every decision we make whether we like it or not. The cycle must stop somewhere why not with you? Until you can wake up and face reality and face your problems then you can never fully take full control of your actions. You must be willing to make peace with your past hurt, disappointments, defeats, and if not, there will be no way you can move past those things. Your past can deter you from everything you've always desired.

LOST AND UNDEVELOPED CHILD

I carried the hurt of my father not being in my life until I was 24 years old, I am now 26 years old. I know what you are thinking WOW! that's a long time. Yes, I know, and I hated every bit of it. I was angry with him because I wanted to learn from him and for him to be there not just physically but spiritually and mentally. I wanted to know what it took to be a man, how to become a man, and what a man even looked like. I wanted him to be there so bad and teach me how to be a man and give me the knowledge to help me conquer the world as other fathers did for their children. I grew a bitterness feeling towards him which turned to HATE and was disgusted every time someone would say his name. I even started to hate my own name because I was named after him.

I once had a conversation with someone, and they told me "The more I hold on to this the more complicated my life will be and the more I will be hurt and struggle". I eventually concluded that I was the one holding up my own life. Sometimes in life we must be our own best friend and be real with ourselves to reach our full potential. You have some teens who are reaching out to us, but we ignore them, so they seek validation and direction from drug dealers, gangs, drugs, etc. as their guidance counselors and mentors in life. Therefore, we must look ourselves in the mirror and make peace with our past. so that we can pass along the right message and to the next generation to come.

Chapter 2

THE ABSENT DAD

As parents we must do better by being there for our children. Not only physically but mentally and spiritually. Life can be a rollercoaster, and some may want to give in and others may want to embrace the ride. How you handle the ride will speak volumes about your life and yourself. Fathers leaving their children's lives has become a huge issue in today's world. The crazy thing about it is that it's not just a one state issue its worldwide. "More than 20 million children live in a home without the physical presence of a father. Millions more have dads who are physically present, but emotionally absent. If it were classified as a disease, fatherlessness would be an epidemic worthy of attention as a national emergency" (The Extent of Fatherlessness - National Center for

Fathering, 2022). Maybe this is for you or someone you may know. If you never heard these words, I just want to say from the bottom of my heart "I'm sorry your father left you, I'm sorry he couldn't be the man you wanted him to be, I'm sorry for all the hurt and pain he caused you". You probably even look at other Individuals who have their father and get sad. How do I know? because that was me. I can relate because I went through the same thing. As I stated earlier my father was in and out my life since and early age. I really needed my father like most young kids do.

When you become a teen, you go through puberty which calls for your body and perspective on a lot of things to change. This had made it difficult because I had no clue what these changes were. When my father left, I felt worthless inside. I felt as if a child lost his favorite toy, and everything was chaos. I thought of my father as my hero like many other kids who think their father is the strongest and toughest man around. Here I was, a young teen with no father, laying in a dark room crying and asking myself "When is daddy coming back". I had no role model to look up to, no male figure to look up to just my mom.

Having my mother around was amazing but as a young boy you want to grow a bond with your father and be able to play ball or watch games with him. I started to get attached to other men and hurting myself even more because they would leave too. I was facing an abandonment issue I had no clue about. Dads fill a different void in a child's life that a mother just can't fill, no matter how great she is as a parent. Sons need a father to teach them how to grow from a boy to a man and demonstrate a great character within themselves. Daughters also need their fathers in their lives. They need a father who's going to show them a good example of what a man is, and how a man is supposed to treat them. Some women see their fathers beating on their mother and leading by example in a negative way. This in return causes them to think that this is what men are supposed to do to them. They tend to not understand men or how to deal with one because they don't even know how to understand and deal with their own father.

A girls first love is always her father and the majority of time their father is also always their first heartbreak. When young girls grow up with a bad example of a father, they often times settle for damaged men because that is what they were taught. I never understood my father because how can you abandoned a child you gave not only your first name to but your whole name to. I was another version of him, but I guess that didn't matter. Out of all my 26 years of living I don't remember my father ever teaching me something positive. My father was into the drug game and living a lifestyle that wasn't any good for him. I used to ride with him while he made his "plays." I used to watch him in the kitchen making things that I had no business watching and seeing things that weren't good for my eyes. I had a half brother and sister from my dad's side. My sister normally wouldn't be present when my dad was doing these things, mostly because he wanted to protect her. In my head I didn't understand because I also didn't want to be around it either. Watching him live a broken lifestyle caused me to never want to live this same lifestyle when I got older. .

Having an absent father sometimes meant he would miss out on important events in my life. I want to share a short conversation between my father and I because this memory always stays with me.

A Conversation Between me and my dad:

Me: "Hey dad, I have my 9th grade basketball game at Coloma High School at 5 o'clock PM against Edwardsburg."

Him: "Ok, son you know I will be there."

Me: "Ok dad I can't wait. I'm going to ball out for you I'm going to make you so proud!"

Him: "Ok Son see you tomorrow."

Me: "Bye Dad."

I was so pumped that my dad was finally going to see me play in a real game. I was so excited I barely could sleep that night. The excitement continued all night until gametime. I felt like I drank a million energy drinks because I couldn't stop moving around. I couldn't sit down from being excited and ready to give my father something to be proud of. It was finally game time and my teammates and I are in our lay-up line. It's ten minutes to tip-off and no sign of my dad. I had no worries because I knew he wasn't going to let me down. I just continue to warm up and focus. As the ten minutes expired my dad still hadn't shown up. I figured he might be running a little late. I go out and dominate the first three minutes hitting two three pointers back-to-back but unfortunately this didn't continue. I looked into the stands to see where my father was but there was no sign of him. As I looked into the stands the offensive player scored right in my face. I then proceeded to dribble the ball up the court. I looked back again and no sign . This time the ball was stolen from me, and a fast break point was scored. I let my father's absence distract me the entire game.

My coach kept telling me to get my head in the game and focus. I knew I needed to let it go and focus too but, I just wanted him there to see his son ball. Why didn't he come? All the other kid's fathers were there cheering for them and mine wasn't. All these bad thoughts had my emotions high, and I continued to turn the ball over as I looked into the stands and miss shots going into halftime. My coach Thomas gave us a halftime speech and went over the second half game plan. After leaving the locker room he said to me, "What the heck was going on out there? I have never seen you play like this." I then told him the story and conversation with my father. His response was "We can't force everyone in our life to show up, but we can show up for ourselves". This was so true! You can't force someone to be there, but you can choose to be there and show up for your own life.

I went out and played well during the third quarter and ended up scoring ten points. The fourth quarter rolled around, and we are up by six points. Edwardsburg made six straight points and our coached then went to call a timeout. I looked over at the stands just to see if my dad so happened to be there but no, I was still left disappointed. Its' two minutes left and we're up four points. We were securing the lead, holding the ball and wasting time on the clock. A whole minute goes by and we missed the shot. Edwardsburg goes down and make two shots back-to-back. The game is now tied 40-40. I come down the court with the ball and tried to hurry up and get the ball out my hands but was fouled quickly. I looked into the stands and didn't see my father. I missed not one but both free throws. Edwardsburg stalled and took time off the clock and went up for lay-up and got fouled. They went to make one free throw out of two. The score is now 41-40. I get the ball and a wide-open rim is what I see. I go for a lay-up but OH NO! It's blocked! I go back to the line with confidence I did my normal routine and made the first one YES! Another timeout was called. I then go back to the line with the game tied 41-41 and a chance to win. I always dreamed of this moment so, here I go with the chance to make my dream come true. I get the ball from the ref, I dribble twice and looked one last time to see if my father was in the stands. I told him I wanted to make him proud, and this one shot could do it by icing the game. I go to take the shot and miss! I was so frustrated with myself and accidentally fouled.

I couldn't even wait to we get to the locker room and tears started bawling from my face because I had the chance to win the game, but I let my father's absence stop me. We went to lose 42-41. This game was an example of my relationship with my father. He was always making promises he couldn't keep. I always blamed myself, and let his absence ruin me for days. Every time I would see kids with their father at parks, dads cheering for their son at games, etc. I would always get teary eyed because that's all I ever wanted was to grow a bond with my father that was unbreakable. I would go over my friends Jason, Kevin and Caleb' houses and seen how they had both parents in the house and get sad. I never let it show though. Their fathers always came to their games rooting and cheering for them. The more I hung around them I started to feel jealous because I wanted what they had. Their mom and dad always treated me like family and I appreciated them for that but it made me feel even worse because nobody knew how bad I was hurting and dying on the inside without the presence of my own father.

After my father was out of the drug game, he told me "What you want me to do? Go back to jail? I can't buy you the things you want" I see now that he was lost and didn't understand me because all I wanted was just my father to be there. It's never about the money that you spend on a child its always about the time spent. You can give a child a million toys, but the toys can break, they can outgrow them, but time a child is always going remember who was there and all the memories that was created. I was never an ungrateful kid. I remember Christmas one year we didn't have much and my mom brought me just books for Christmas and I was so happy. So, for him to say that hurt even more because it wasn't about the expensive things for me, I just wanted the simple things such as him being there for me like other fathers was there for their kids. I have felt unwanted and unloved my whole life. They say a father can be a girls first heartbreak, but it can also be a young boys first heartbreak because my father was mine.

Chapter 3

HEARTBREAK

---

*Have you ever been so happy with your
life you feel like it was so good to be true?
Have you ever faced a heartbreak, or someone left your life it made you turn blue?
Have you ever loved someone so bad
it made you look like a fool?*

—Robert Lawson

Being in-love is one of the greatest feelings in this world when you are loved correctly. You ever loved someone, and everything is so perfect and nothing can seem to go wrong? That was me! I was 15 in the 9th grade when I thought I met the love of my life Mira. Only a few percent of couples make it out to become high school sweethearts and she always told me we were that few percent. I was so happy to meet her and get to know her. Once I got to know her it was like we were so perfect for each other. She was 5'2 same size as me, black hair, brown skin, brown eyes and everything I always wanted. We had so much in common and could talk for hours without getting bored we would stay up all night talking about our future, goals, dreams and so many other things. We would even fall asleep on the phone all night until the morning. We would go on dates, church, water parks, walks on the beach and so much more. She gave me the love I always wanted to feel as a young boy. She was giving me the love that I always wanted from my father.

Nobody wants to feel lonely or empty inside so we try and fill that empty void with all the love we can get. When I met Mira, it was like I was a college athlete who got drafted to the pros. It felt like a new life, excitement, and relief. She inspired me to be a great person and pushed me to be even better. She always wanted better for me and that's when I started to fall in love with her. She was smart, funny, pretty, great personality, and most of all she loved me. I risked a lot for her because I wanted to feel needed, supported, and loved. Her flaws didn't bother me they were beautiful in their own way. There wasn't a day where I didn't think about her. I loved her, wanted her, and needed to hear her voice. We were together for five years and in those years there was a lot of good memories made. We had so much fun together and what made it even better is that her family loved me. They always told me how great of a young boy I was and loved the way I treated her. We knew each other like the back of our hands. We knew when each other was mad, sad, happy, and knew everything about each other. . I treated her like royalty, like a queen, and paved the grounds she walked on. I know you are probably thinking if it was this amazing then why did she leave? Your guess is as good as mines.

Aside from the good times ,there was a lot of bad times as well. Like normal couples there was arguing, cheating, hurtful words, disappointments, and lies. She had me in so deep that I didn't see any other girl but her. I craved her not in a sexual way but just how she made me feel like I can conquer the world. I felt like I was the luckiest guy in the world who went to the store got a ticket scratch off and won millions of dollars. That is how she made me feel. It felt like I was a kid all over again on the merry go round just happy and full of joy. Everything was good until the cheating and lies started. I caught her cheating and texting other guys. I was disappointed because out of all people I wouldn't expect for her to do that. She had me in so deep that she told me she was sorry, and it won't happen again. And of course after some days I took her back and just like that everything went back to normal. Each time a little cautious but not cautious enough. I got into an argument with my cousin because he told me I was dumb, stupid, and blind to see what was going on. She just always knew what to say. Always knew how to make me feel better.

She was my biggest fan and supporter. She always came to my games, the same games I was looking for my father to come to. Months later my cousin finally wrote me again and said I must tell you something. He called me and said, "Your girlfriend is cheating on you". I told him You are just jealous, leave us alone." After months of us not talking, this time he sends me proof. In a couple of the messages she was telling this guy that she has no boyfriend and we didn't go to prom together. She also sent a guy a naked photo of herself which she denied instantly. However, I knew it was her because of her fingers and nail polish blue which she had on. After I pointed that out, she admitted to it being true. I knew it was time to leave but I fell even harder but this time for potential. I fell in love with the young lady I knew she could be and really felt that it would all stop. I was naïve and thought that we would somehow still live happily ever after. No matter how much you and a person fix things you will always think back to how they did you wrong. It's tough to love a person who didn't value you the first time.

One day I snuck her over my aunt house. We chilled ,watched movies and had fun. As she went to the bathroom someone by the name of "Pooh" called. I handed her, her phone, but she didn't answer it. I didn't think of anything because I didn't want to argue and just wanted to continue to have fun. She went to the restroom again and this time her phone rings again back-to-back. I answered it for her thinking it was emergency and it was a guy who she had been talking to. I asked her about him and she denied. He called back trying to talk crazy to me. My feelings were hurt, and I did something that I never did before and I hit her multiple times. It was like it was a whole bunch of anger and frustration built up inside because I was tired of the lies, the cheating, I was tired of everything and everyone. The most dangerous type of anger is built inside someone with a good heart. We get used to being taken advantage of and it's so frustrating, and the frustration turns to tears and tears turn to anger and anger turns to rage. Then when we finally snap, and we are left looking like we're crazy. People with good hearts get tired too. I hated it with every bit of me. It

We must pay attention to the red flags and stop trying to pray them away.

was like she was turning me into something I wasn't. I had never hit a woman before. This was my first and only time. I begged God for forgiveness I begged God for guidance and a way out. I was so hurt ,lost and confused. I sat in my room and cried for so long praying and begging God to help me to leave this relationship. She kept pulling me in like a fish on a fishing pole.

One sunny afternoon I was home alone and I was extremely frustrated with myself for what I did. I was frustrated with my dad, frustrated at God, frustrated with everyone. I went to my mom's room and grabbed her gun, I wrote my suicidal letter, sent pictures to loved ones and told them bye. As I go to lift the gun up and attempt to commit suicide, I press the trigger and was ready for the consequences. However, the gun jammed. I tried to fix it again and it jammed again. I was so frustrated with God but he's the one who just saved me. Sometimes we may think God isn't listening, but he will save you and be right on time just like he was with me. God's timing doesn't have to always make sense but its right on. You must trust him beyond your own understanding. See me I didn't trust God at all because how can a God let my father leave me and let me suffer for so many years. How can a God let me love someone to the point where I lost myself and I no longer knew who I was anymore? One day I was on social media, and I see her post random initials. I asked her who those initials belonged to and she told me it was going to be her son's initials. So, the next couple of days I was on FaceTime with Mira. We were talking, laughing, and having a good old conversation. She was getting all cute. She did her hair, put on some cute clothes, and was looking so beautiful just like the first time I seen her. I asked her where she was going, and she told me she is going on a date with her "gay best friend". A best friend I never knew she had. I knew something about this sounded odd but I didn't want to jump to conclusions. I told my cousin about it, but he told me I was overthinking it and advised me to relax.

However, I thought to myself how could I relax when I'm on the verge of losing something I don't want to lose. When you really love someone, you know when something isn't right or seems off. Always trust and listen to your intuition. With that being said, its 9pm and I still haven't heard from her and this isn't like her. I'm pacing the floors nervous and scared. I then see her post on snapchat a photo of herself hugging and kissing this guy and updated her status to in a relationship on Facebook. I am crushed, hurt, and heartbroken. I didn't even know what to think, say, or go on about life. I tried to reach out to someone for advice: mom, father, uncles, aunts, but no one answered. I was in a dark basement crying, sad, frustrated with life. All I ever wanted was to be loved, feel loved, and every time I'm left with a bigger whole in my heart. All I see is pills, bleach, and more pills. I grabbed the pills took half the bottle and cried, then procced to take more pills and cried some more.

When I took the pills and shallowed them I saw good and evil. It felt like God and the devil were talking to me at the same time. God was asking me why I was doing this you have so much to live for. The pain was hurting so bad it felt like the devil was telling me go take more pills and get it over with the pains will end soon. All of the pain I was feeling was overtaken by all the good I was feeling. I started to take a couple more pills and instantly started to feel nauseous and felt drowsy. It was like my body was telling me to shut down. When I felt my body start to slip away I started to pray right away. Something was telling me to just pray and so I did just that. I prayed "Lord whatever you have in store for me please let me get through this please. Show me the way. Please give me a second chance at life." I really started changing my mind because I felt my soul leaving my body and started feeling numb and that scared me. I prayed some more. I never really wanted to kill myself I just wanted the pain to subside. My prayer really saved my life and God really brought me through that traumatic experience. I slept the whole next day I thought it had worked. I slept from morning to night and still nobody has checked on me or returned my call. Woke up at 2 in the morning my throat was sore, and I couldn't eat at all. I was having real bad hot flashes and laid back down and slept some more.

In life we are taught when we are hurting or have a scar to put a band-aid on it. The only difference is this pain you can't cover it with a band-aid. The bleeding is internal and feels like it's never going to stop. It's like I had to have surgery but was too late because I was drowning in my own blood. People kept telling me it was her loss and my father's loss. They missed out on a great person. But was it really? Because in the end I was the one left alone and miserable. They were out living their best lives while I was still hoping for a text, call or anything that would validate that they cared. Could it possibly be their loss when they made it look like they never lost anything?

No one prepared me for this moment, nor did anyone coach me about girls, heartbreaks, or relationships. All I knew is that I loved someone and felt so empty and hopeless inside. I cried and cried for hours which eventually turned into days. And as time went on I realized this pain carried on months and years. I had thoughts running through my head such as: "Why God why did you allow this to happen to me, why did you allow me to love this person knowing I'll be hurt, why did you let her break me, damage me, and destroy me, WHY GOD?!' I just didn't understand why I wasn't good enough. I felt like an old beat up used car that had no value or purpose left. She always told me I can do and be anything in this world, that I had a calling and a purpose. I started to question everything she ever told me and thought those was lies too. I lost myself, I lost my self-esteem, I felt like I had no purpose, or drive to do anything.

It felt like my father burned me down and she put out the fire. When Mira left it felt like my father left all over again. It was like I was facing two heartbreaks at once. Watching her love someone else like I always wanted her to love me just did something to me. I begged for her love and attention, begged her not to go, and to watch her give that same love I begged for and do all the things we talked about with the next person felt so terrible and wrong. You can't make someone stay; you can't make someone see what a blessing you are. Sometimes you just have to let them miss out and see for themselves.

When you meet someone who really loves and adores you, you will not have to tell them how to treat you. You will no longer cry, you won't be up all night wondering if they are cheating, you won't have to ask how they feel. They will simply show it. Love doesn't hurt. Love is worth fighting for but you can't be the only one fighting. There comes a point where you have to walk away and let it be.

Chapter 4

FEELING LIKE A FAILURE

When I was younger, I would always think I was going to the NBA or NFL nobody could tell me otherwise. I would even sleep with a football or basketball in my hand thanks to my little brothers father Sinatra. If it wasn't for him, I wouldn't know anything about sports. He taught me everything I know. I remember when my New Orleans Saints won the super bowl he was hating because his bears didn't win the superbowl that year. We watched a lot of games together, played sports together, he came to my games supported me in every way he could, and it was all fun, but he wasn't my dad. No matter how much fun I had with a male figure in my life it just brings me down because I wanted it to be my father not someone's else father. I was very grateful for him because he instilled a lot into me until this day. Even when my mother and him didn't work out, he always stayed in touch, and we talked almost every day.

I knew I was going to the pros and I had no back up plan. It wasn't until 11th grade where my mom told me what I should do. I didn't do well on the ACT test as I scored really low. She told me I should go to the Army or the Air Force in my head it sounded good but that's not what I wanted to do. I was just so unprepared for everything and I felt behind. I remember cheating on a math test and getting caught. The teacher told me I wouldn't become anything but another black statistic and end up in jail. This wasn't anything new a lot of people told me that and I wasn't going to the pros because I was too short, or that I would end up on the block selling drugs. There will be a lot of people who will tell you that you cannot do anything but don't listen to them. You can do all things through Christ who strengthens you! Anything is possible with God on your side.

You must go after the life you want, or you will be stuck living a life you can't escape from. There are no limits. We can't listen to teachers, parents, friends etc.

Just dream, believe, and take action. I wish I had someone teaching me these things. I became a believer in negative thoughts and I started to act out. I would skip class, cheat on tests, and not do my homework. Instead of proving everyone wrong, I was proving them right. My A's turned into F's. I was declining so fast. My mom kept pushing me into joining the Army. I went to take the ASVAB practice exam and I failed it. My mom was so disappointed in me and it made me feel like a loser and a failure. So, I went back to take the test again except this time I cheated on it . And guess what, I passed the practice test. My mom was so happy, and her smile was the biggest I had ever seen in years. It is crazy to me that I had to lie just to see that smile and happy side of her.

I then went to take the real test in Lansing Michigan. She was so happy and she knew I was going to pass. Nervous thoughts ran through my mind as I bit my nails. I finished the test and I was so confident in myself and knew I would pass. Unfortunately, I scored a 15 and failed. I was so devastated. You need a passing score of 32 or higher and I wasn't even close. I cried because I wanted to make my mom proud and felt like a failure. I came home and showed my mom, and she was so disappointed in me, but she didn't show it this time. She bought me cards and books to study for the test. After months of studying, I went back to take the test again and failed once more. Even though my mom wanted me to go to the Army so bad I felt like she was pushing me to do something I truly wasn't passionate about and it was hurting me in the long run. I was losing confidence in myself and caught myself believing all the negative thoughts about myself. I was trying so hard to make my mom happy and the more I tried, I started to become unhappy myself. If we continue to do what our parents what us to do it ultimately will never make us happy. This time my mom got me a tutor and more materials to study with. Months passed by again and took the test one last time. I thought I passed but I failed once again. I didn't know what I was doing wrong. My mom eventually got to the point where she thought Mira was the cause for my inability to pass. The first time I failed the practice test I got in the car and my mom yelled and said to me "You are not trying to pass because you trying to stay here with that girl. You will never get to where you are going if you keep doing that". Truth be told I wasn't letting her stop me. I just couldn't pass the test because I was not giving it my all.

FEELING LIKE A FAILURE

I was lost and had no sense of direction because I didn't know what was next for my life. All I knew was life was passing me by and I had no clue who I was anymore. I didn't know if I was coming or going. I was questioning myself, thinking how I can stop this feeling. Have you ever caught yourself saying you're not good enough, you're a failure and worthless? You're not alone I have too! You even start to think less about yourself, you doubt yourself, you have negative self-talk, we are what we say. So, if you continue to say those negative things you will eventually become them. We must speak life into our life and to our individual self. "I will be successful; I am not a failure ." and many other positive things. My mother's husband Rocky pushed us to try and enlist in the Army. I met his nephew and we studied together, took practice tests online, and quizzed each other. After months of doing this we went to take the test together. I was confident again and told myself "You will pass, and you are not a failure". I took my time with the test and smiled as I answered the questions while I positively thought to myself how good I was doing. Once I was done I got the final score in an envelope. I walk down the hall open it, and my heart dropped because I failed again! A tear fell down my face. It was a long ride home millions of thoughts were running through my mind. Thoughts of failure, thoughts of giving up, thoughts of I am not good enough. I just didn't understand. I put in so many hours of studying and still failed. I got home and lied to my mother and said I got a higher score than last time but, I got a score of 13. If you thought my mom was disappointed before she was really disappointed this time and this time it was like she was giving signs of giving up.

I felt like she accepted that I would never pass the test. Almost every other day I would hear from my mother's husband Rocky about why he wanted us to go to the Army. I got tired of always hearing about that Army. So, I stopped coming home and started to hang out elsewhere. I can remember one evening, my mom's husband nephew and I went to the Army recruiter's office to schedule the test. The Army recruiter was getting smart with me and was insinuating that if I didn't enlist in the Army, I wouldn't have a successful life. My mom's husband sister looked at me with a smirk as if he was right or as if her son was better because he passed and I didn't. Almost my whole father's side is in the Army but I didn't want to be like them. I wanted to create my own path. That was something my mom told me when I graduated, that I was a model child and not to be afraid. She always reminded me to be myself and create my own path. It didn't seem that way though it was if she was forcing me into something I didn't really want to do.

Have you ever been pressured by someone to do something that you didn't really want to do? That's how I felt deep down inside. I wanted to prove all of them wrong. I wanted them to know that someone doesn't have to go to the Army to be successful. I always knew I had a great gift for helping others. When my grandmother had cancer, we would go over to her house and help her out. This is when I fell in love with the healthcare field by seeing a smile on my grandma's face, I wanted to make others smile that same way. I started doing healthcare work and loved it because I was impacting people lives and making a difference in people lives. My grandma would always praise me for having a kind caring heart like her and always told me I had a higher gift and purpose. I once worked at a job called The Fountains. I met this elderly lady name Mary who was the lady I was caring for at the time. She was very sweet and we built a really nice friendship. My coworkers told me she was mad at me and I didn't know why. So, I went outside to speak with her and she said she heard I was leaving. She didn't want me to leave because I reminded her so much of her son passed away a few years ago and I impacted her life so much in a way no one ever has since he left. She asked if she could give me hug and I accepted. We both shed a tear. That's when I knew God had a purpose for my pain, my struggle, and my life.

Nobody will never understand the vision or dream God placed upon you and that's ok. If God gave you a vision no one but you can stop it from manifesting. Have you ever had a dream and a vision so big, that you mention it to your friends and family and they instantly shoot it down? Most of the time they cannot relate because God sent it for you not them. God put those visions and dreams in your heart and in your mind for a reason. We don't have to tell everyone our dreams and visions because not everyone will understand. The reason we keep imagining that we will be rich, have a nice car, graduate, get the house we dreamed of is because God is talking to us and showing us what he has for us. God is the real deal and we must believe in him and trust his vision for our life. You have to start somewhere and the only person that can stop you is you.

A good exercise that has helped me is making a list of everything I envision for my life. So, what I want you to do is write down everything you imagine, pray about it and watch what happens. No matter how big your vision is don't let anyone stop you because you have what it takes. I always allowed family, friends, and outsiders, to shoot my ideas down so, I know how it feels. But

Failure is what drives us to success.

when you get tired of playing small and being the victim you start to take action and prove them wrong. It all starts with you! So. let today be the first step in into your vision.

Chapter 5

MEN HAVE A VOICE TOO

All of my life I was taught boys don't cry. I was always told I cried too much and was told to be a man. because I was too sensitive, too emotional, and other things you wouldn't imagine. As I got older these thoughts killed me. I would think I wasn't supposed to show any emotion, cry, or even feel sad. I would always portray this hard tough guy feeling holding everything all in. I would hold anger, guilt, tears, fears, and sadness. The more I held on to all of this the more I was causing more built-up pain and anger inside of me. You know when you get a bottle and you put a million chemicals that don't match in that bottle and it get to foaming and raising to the top ready to explode. That was me and my bottle I held everything in it and the more I held things in there the more dangerous it got. I exploded once I reached my breaking point.

As parents we have to do better with telling our children not to cry. Teaching our children at a young age that they are supposed to express their hurt with no tears or emotions can be problematic. We are taught to put the pain to the side, brush it off, or simply forget about it. I can't forget how I was told not to let other guys see me cry because they will laugh at me, call me a sissy, and a punk. This little belief makes it hard for us men to even ask for help or even want help. Women sometimes get mad because we don't ask for help or direction but that's because we will seem weak that we can't figure it out on our own. When we do talk about it often times it gets thrown in our faces and forces us not to open up again. By holding everything in it made me feel like I was all alone and had nobody. My self-worth and myself image started to fade because I started to feel like I wasn't me if I can't do those things. I would question myself and ask, who is the real Robert Lawson? I felt like I couldn't be myself and show emotions and cry. Restraining boys and men to not show emotions will lead to depression and even suicide. It's ok to feel sad because you'll never know what being happy means. It's ok to feel weak because we will never know what it means to be strong. It's ok to cry and it's ok to not be ok. We have emotions just like everyone else believe it or not.

Many times, I wanted to cry, shout, and scream but I felt like I couldn't. I felt like it was my job to be strong. The worse part of being strong is no one really realizes when you are hurting or on the verge of hanging it all up. I had to be strong and stand tall when I was slowly falling apart. All I heard growing up was to be a man but how does one even do that when you have never experienced a real male role model in your life. The man I had seen never really showed emotion either and I repeated the same behaviors. I quickly got tired of it and I wanted to feel heard and noticed. As a man I wanted to be strong and not validated just by what I could provide or what bills I could pay. We need to be provided for us too. Some women look at us as if we are supposed to have it all figured out when they don't even have it all figured out themselves.

What if someone told you a deep intimate story about myself? Would you jump to conclusions and judge me? What if I told you I was sexually abused not once but multiple times and now I try to numb the pain with sex. Would that have led to me being less of a man? This just shows you that men hold a lot in and I decided that I wouldn't do that anymore. Nobody deserves to go through something like this. I sure as hell didn't. A lot of people would NEVER believe me but here is my story. I ended up getting sexually abused by my dad's girlfriend Jessica.

"Shut up" as Jessica told me" I can finally have you to myself'. She procced with telling me that my father was sleeping and told me she liked me and always wanted me. She then took off my clothes and had sex with me. I didn't know what was going on. I never had heard of a boy getting sexually abused. That night I was the victim. I hated my father even more for letting that happen to me, I felt he was supposed to protect me. The next morning, we went home I balled up in the showered and scrubbed my body till I couldn't feel her touching it anymore. The more I scrubbed the more I cried because I could still hear the voices and scene replaying in my mind. A lot of people say I always look sad but nobody knew I was fighting that every single day. Not even my mother or father knew! The more I held it in the more pain it caused.

There were so many times where I wanted to open my heart and tell the world and show emotions but who would've believed? As stated before, we are told to be "strong", be a man and get over it. I did tell a few friends for advice but they just laughed and said what's the problem, your finally not a virgin anymore. I felt that was so pathetic and insensitive. I hated the feeling, so I never told anyone else. Many people thought I simply wanted attention. If it was a female everyone would've believe her. So there was definitely a double standard. That wasn't the case with me everyone stopped talking to me as if I was a liar or an attention seeker. I was left traumatized and suicidal. She took advantage of me and left me broken.

Being damaged started to feel normal to me because that's all I have ever felt and all I kept experiencing was pain and hurt. The most damaging part was keeping this a secret up until now. Being sexually abused at a young age force you to look at things differently and grow up in a different way. Some end up experiencing issues with sex, major trust issues and some even become codependent and end up loving the wrong person too hard. Often times post-traumatic stress occurs and the victim may even live in fear that it might happen again. After this situation I became codependent and was looking for love in all the wrong places. I started to get addicted to sex and turned into a sex addict. I didn't know that I deserved to be treated the right way. I blamed myself for it even though it was out of my control. I'm happy to say I'm survivor of it. I used to consider myself a victim but now I'm a survivor.

I know it's hard and there are days where you just sitting in a room under the covers scared of the dreams and the flash backs. It ate me alive all my life because it didn't just happen once, it happened multiple times. Every time I would close my eyes all I could here is "shut up you are ok". So, when people tell me "Shut up" that just triggers everything and I just shut down. People used to ask me what's wrong after saying it and I wouldn't say anything. Men are so used to doing the crime that it shocked people when you tell them it's the other way around so in return nobody believes us. To everyone reading this, if someone touches you inappropriately, say something. Sexual assault is a crime, no matter who does it. It is not okay! Make sure to speak to someone, tell someone, and get it off your chest.

Chapter 6

LOVED BUT NOT LOVED

All my life I always felt like I was alone. I always wanted to feel loved. I looked at how other friends and people were so close to their parents and I always got sad because I wasn't that close to mine. I wasn't close to my dad at all and when we did hang out, he was making his drug deals or with a female. We did go-carting a lot but that was something my sister always wanted to do not me. I was always jealous to a lot of kids my age who could run to their parents whenever they have a problem. Many of times I asked myself how does it feel to cry in your moms lap or father arms while talking about your day,? I grew up without my parents knowing their little boy was fighting so many demons and it felt so alone at night. People always told me to be grateful that I at least had one parent. I am very grateful for my mother. She did everything for me and my little brother all by herself. She was a single parent and made it look easy. She managed to put clothes on our backs, food on table, and roof over heads with no problem at all. Or at least that's how she made it seem. She was a good parent and yes, she was there physically but at least for me when it came to the emotional support, she just wasn't there. She might think she was but, it didn't feel like it. My mom was the parent where she didn't let anyone see her weakness, see her cry, or really show a lot of emotion. I couldn't talk to my mom about certain things. She would tell me "Robert get out my face with that" or "you're too sensitive". Maybe she always thought I was playing because I always had a goofy personality. I hated it because I had no one to share my feelings with or to talk to me. I had a total of five uncles. The first uncle was in the streets and was never really around. The second uncle was facing his own problems within himself so I couldn't really talk to him. Two other uncles were still living with my grandma at the time and they were trying to find out how to be men themselves. The last uncle was found about a couple years ago so I didn't know much of him. He was estranged since I was very little. Every child needs good loving connections to turn into an healthy overall human being. My mother was playing both roles in my life as a mother and a father. She cooked, cleaned, worked, and took care of my little brother and myself. I never once seen her complain or give up and although I could tell she was tired. She was working so hard to provide for us and live her life at the same time. She was providing physically but when it came to emotionally it just seems like there was something missing. I didn't feel comfortable with telling her certain things or just didn't feel the emotional connection. Most of the time it felt like she wasn't even interested so I would never say anything. I would hold everything in and suffer in silence which wasn't good at all. This made me go look for the approval elsewhere. I started to look towards other older adults for love since I was not getting that from my mom and dad. I started to look for it in girls and ended up with girls who didn't really like me. Even my so-called friends were making it seem like nobody else wanted to be my friend and they're the only friends I would ever have. I had no self-value or self-worth and started to listen to everybody else's judgement and slowly started to forget who I was at the moment. All of this started to show up more when I moved out of my mother's home and it started to affect how I saw myself.

My mom had to step up as my father my entire life. It wasn't fair how she had done double the work but she made it look so easy. She never once complains about it. The love my mom showed was tough love. She was hard on us because she always wanted something great for us. She pushed us every day and made sure we were on the right path. My mom did an amazing job raising us although it was hard at times. My mom always hid her feelings and after getting to know her story I realized why she was the way she is. Sometimes that's all it takes is having a conversation and realizing our parents' story. My mom had it hard growing up and she didn't want that for us. I am the oldest out of my mom 's three children and personally I felt like I had it the worse. I would always get whooping's and get yelled at. My younger brother wouldn't really get yelled at like me and never got hit. My mom didn't really let me stay out late or go to homecoming dances but when I graduated, she allowed my younger brother to. I started to feel like she loved him more and showed more love towards him than me. She would always tell me to stop being jealous of my younger brother but I wasn't. I was just expressing how I was seeing it. It felt like she was prouder of him than me. I always wanted to make my mom proud and felt like I wasn't doing that. She never really told me she was proud of me. So, I was seeking for her validation in everything I did. I got into with my mom really bad. We both said things we didn't mean. I went months without talking to her. I called every one of my aunts and uncles and I asked if I was wrong . Each one told me that's just how your mom is. I then called my grandma and told her everything, she agreed that I wasn't wrong but told me to apologize. I laughed and I said, "grandma are you serious after all she said and you want me to apologize?" She told me life is too short, you said what you had to in order to get it off your chest. Your mom had it hard growing up from the things I did and all that she went through." I was sad when she told me that. So, I went and apologized to my mom after months of not speaking. After that, my relationship with my mom became closer. She is an amazing woman that makes me drive to do more for myself every day! She made me realize I can do anything I put my mind to! She's the epitome of what a beautiful, hard working woman and mother should be! She has set the tone for our entire family, immediate and extended! I strive to be everything that she is! I know if no one else in this world has my back, she definitely does!

Chapter 7

BECOMING A FATHER

I have three children named Jay'Dion, Josiah, and Jaliyah. Two kings and one princess. Becoming a father was one of the greatest things life has ever given me after all the pain and hurt. To make it even better they all are by one person and that person is my wife, Danielle. I had my first son June of 2018, and I finally had the chance to get a taste of what fatherhood was all about. All of my life I felt like I was just living to be living with no purpose and no drive. It's a sweet feeling to actually live for someone else and that person will call you dad for a lifetime. I went from living my life day to day and it evolved. I now have the opportunity to love, to be a teacher, a mentor, father, a provider, and a leader. A lot of people told me I wasn't ready to become a father.

TRIAL AND ERROR

There will be a lot of people who will tell you you're not ready for a lot of things but if you listen to them, you'll never be ready. I remember it like it was yesterday. I had gone to work and I wasn't even there for more than 3 hours and I got a call from her stating that she's having bad contractions and its time. My anxiety went up the roof because now I'm really going to be a father. I got a ride to the hospital and she was 2cm dilated and all I could do is pace the hospital floors anxious and ready. As hours went by she dilated from 2cm to 4cm to 7cm. Then it was time to push! Doctors rush in and got in their spots and all I hear is push, push, push and push! The baby got halfway down the birth canal and I just couldn't believe that I could see his head full of hair. Contractions are coming back-to-back and with a few more pushes the baby is finally here. I couldn't believe it I was finally a father. I heard my son's first cry. It was so nice and scary at the same time because it was so loud like thunder. I got scared because he stopped breathing for a while and they had to take him immediately. Relief came after doctors came into the room and said he was fine. One of the best feelings is when I was finally able to hold, feel, see, him for the very first time.

BECOMING A FATHER

I just knew I was going to be the best father ever but yet there was still some doubt and nervousness. I kept asking myself are you really ready? Could I even change a pamper? Can I handle it all? I wasn't sure about none of these things but I wouldn't let that stop me from trying. Changing a pamper was easy, bathing them was easy, being there was easy. But it was the sleepless nights, the crying, the fussing for no reason that made it difficult. It was hard and a big adjustment I had to get used to. How could you provide for your little one when you could barely provide for yourself. How could I be their when I could barely be there for myself. I never had the person to show me what it took to be a dad. All I knew was what a father shouldn't do. I was scared when I really thought about it because I didn't want to make the same mistakes my father made with me.

The more I thought about it the more I started to not do good as a father. I would be mean, yell for no reason, push them away, and get frustrated. I didn't like that because I was starting to turn into everything I didn't want to be. People would tell me my life was over once I started to have kids. I know a lot of people probably told you the same thing but that isn't true.

That's when your life begins. That's when I felt I had a reason and a why in life. It wasn't about me anymore it was about them. I thought I had to give up everything but if you adjust then it can work. I thought I had to quit school but unfortunately I didn't have to. It's okay to build an empire with a baby or few on your hip. Babies are blessings and can be your biggest motivation. Don't let someone make you feel bad for how many children you have. You can still accomplish everything you want with a child. The only person that can hold you back is yourself. Children don't slow you down they give you purpose. There were so many times, where I wanted to quit and give up. So many times, I cried and my children were right there saying "daddy what's wrong" and wiping my tears. So many times, I cried when they were there and they had no clue what was going on. Those silent cries as a parent hit hard the most. I say that because no matter how drained you feel, exhausted you are, the day you are not feeling good, or just have a lot on your plate, you just can't give up. It's our job to wipe our tears, put our daddy or mommy capes on and continue with our duties. For any parent going through tough times, keep going, and don't give up. It gets better with time. Our children are watching us and to them we are super mom and super dad, we are they heroes.

I tried committing suicide one time because I felt like a failure. I felt I could barely provide for myself, how was I going to provide for them. I had to remember that I have three beautiful babies looking up to me. I didn't want them looking up to anyone else so I had to figure this father thing out. A lot of people didn't think I would make it and most of them gave up on me. but God didn't give up on me and ultimately I didn't give up on myself. Statistics show just only a few percent of students who have children completes a bachelor's degree. I didn't let that statistic stop me. "Only 18% of student parents actually earn an associate's or bachelor's degree within six years, a problem that not only affects their own long-term economic stability, but that of their kids, too" (Silcox, 2022). I proved everyone wrong.

This fatherhood journey was so challenging and stressful at times. I started college in 2017 at Lake Michigan College and it was challenging. I was always late to my classes because I had no ride and had to take the city bus. They eventually rescinded my financial aid. I ended up having to drop my classes after the second semester. Yes, I was discouraged because I was trying to give my children a better life and someone to be proud of. It was only a small setback for a better comeback. A year later after my son was born, I tried it again but this time I got a job and they helped pay for my courses through the University of Phoenix. I signed up and got accepted. I overcame all the obstacles thrown my way and finish the year strong. As I entered my junior year of college, I found out that my wife was pregnant with baby number two. However, I stopped working at the job and the college tuition reimbursement ended. So, I had to start paying out of pocket in order to finish my degree. I had to put my children's needs first. Just two years after that my wife was pregnant again with our baby girl. All of those who were on praying on my downfall were probably happy now. However, we serve an amazing God and through all the trials and tribulations I still made it through. I went on to finish my four-year degree in three years and graduated a whole year early I was supposed to graduate on June 2022 but graduated early on November 21, 2021 with my bachelor's degree in Healthcare Administration.

BECOMING A FATHER

I wouldn't be where I am today if it wasn't for my children. So, let this be a reminder to you that whatever you say you want to do in life, put your mind to it and make it happen. Don't let anyone discourage you, let this be your motivation. Everyone has a testimony to tell. With God on your side and the right mindset, belief and faith you can accomplish anything you want in life. Dream big. Become that person who you always wanted to be when you were growing up.

Chapter 8

MY DEPRESSION

"At its worst, depression can lead to suicide. Over 700,000 people die due to depression each year. Suicide is the fourth leading cause of death"(Depression 2021). Depression is not talked about like it should. Most people don't take depression as serious as they should. I saw a post on Facebook where someone mentioned that they hated when people go on there to talk about death or suicide. They hated that energy and it made them want to delete those types of people. Everyone is not blessed with a good life and can't control what happens to them. This is why a lot of people commit suicide. Mental health is extremely important. You will never fully be yourself if your mental health is not stable and balanced.

TRIAL AND ERROR

My depression made me feel like I was a part of one of those scary movies where someone gets kidnapped and trapped inside a dark basement. I felt like I was chained up for years. I had no light and my power inside of me completely went out. Depression sometimes looks like lying-in bed all day, going without eating, not showering right away, wanting to be alone, and feeling alone. I would get depressed out of nowhere sometimes, I instantly felt unloved, unwanted and unappreciated all at once! I started thinking about death, the people I love that I lost and felt immense pain! I felt drained and annoyed at times. I always wanted to sit in my room in the dark and I always feel like crying for no reason. I would get sad because no matter how hard you try no one will ever fully understand because you barely understand what's happening yourself. A million thoughts and emotions go through your mind all at once. I couldn't explain any of it I just kept praying to God every day that I get back to myself. I was living and fighting a depression inside my body. I was trying so hard to survive while fighting demons and thoughts in my head that tried to push me to kill myself.

MY DEPRESSION

My depression started when I was in the sixth grade. My mom would cut my hair but she would cut it kind of bald and most kids would call me murderer. I would go to school and the kids would make fun of me and slap the back of my head. Here I am bending over getting my books out my locker and next thing you know kids are smacking the back of my head causing all of my books to fall. As I attempt to pick them up they would smack the back of my head again. There were times I couldn't wait for school to end so I could get home. I eventually started to hate school and started to act out and get suspended until my hair grew back. I used to go home and cry because I didn't deserve that. This became an everyday thing and every day I started to feel like I was at war. I used to get beat up, jumped and always tried to fight back. Most days I would hide in the bathroom to avoid getting pick on but it didn't work. They always found me there too.

Now as an adult, when I go to the bathroom in public places, I still get flashbacks on how I used to get beat up and how many times my head hit the bathroom floors. I used to beg for help. There were plenty of times where I wanted to tell someone but I was so afraid because they told me if I tell anyone it'll get worse. So, I took it and tried to deal with it the best I could. That didn't help much because the more I experienced this, the more I wanted to die and kill myself. Kids would even make fun of my height and call me a midget, mini leprechaun and a dwarf. When I would go into public places I would look around and see who would be the first to say something. It was never one person; it was always multiple people who would say something. They would ask me how old I was and say it was cute. They were trying to be funny but, it really was cruel and rude. It felt like I wasn't a human or an ugly made-up creature. Deep down inside I was crying and wishing I was someone else. I was wishing I was taller, and better looking. How they felt about me is how I started to feel about myself. People would treat me like being short was a crime but whole time they were the ones doing the crime by bullying me. At school I was even put in trash cans because they thought I was too short to get out. I started to hate my life, and everything about it. I thought I knew what pain was by not having a father and dealing with the other things I went through in life.

Depression is a different type of pain though. It felt like someone took the sun from the sky and left nothing but dark clouds and lightning with a big tornado ahead. After going through all these events, I started to isolate myself. I felt down, unhappy, lazy, and just this constant sadness that wouldn't leave. The depression started off with being sad for a day, and then it turned into weeks. Eventually it became months. As the days went by the feelings and sadness wouldn't go away and they only got deeper and deeper. It felt like if someone dug a deep hole and put me in there. It was difficult to enjoy my life. I felt like I was chained to my bed and had no idea how to get out.

I also didn't know that my skin color could have a huge impact on my depression as well. I say that because black people are less likely to receive treatment or tell anyone. Going through depression I was just trying to numb the pain with sex, drugs, pills, and a lot of different things. What hurt me more than anything is I tried to give everyone signs but nobody caught them. I wanted to feel loved and cared for. I wanted to feel something! Eventually I started cutting myself. I started cutting on myself because it gave me something to feel. The numbness took away all the thoughts I had because sometimes it was too much for me to bear with. Cutting is not a solution nor is it healthy and is something I no longer do. Family and a lot of my friends felt they knew me but they didn't know the real me. Nobody knows how many times I've lost hope and cried in my room when nobody was looking. Nobody knows how many times I was hurt and abused. Nobody knows when I was on the verge of snapping but just didn't say anything for the benefit of others. Nobody knew the thoughts that went through my head when I was sad. I was so messed up on the inside, fighting silent battles. I was going through it, fake smiling all day and nobody ever knew. To Those fighting silent battles keep going, find what you are destined to do, find something that keep you happy, and most importantly seek God. Ask for strength especially on the days where it gets hard. Whatever you do, don't give up. God will help you go from that dark place to a beautiful place of brightness. I used to post sad stuff on Facebook all the time to try and give family hints nobody ever asked me what was going on. No one inquired about how I was doing, or what they could do to help. The only thing I was ever told was to stop posting sad stuff on Facebook and get my life together. How did they want me to listen to their judgement when they didn't even want to sit down and listen to my problems or to see what was really going on with me.

Check on your loved ones and friends even if you think they're doing ok. A smile can hide so much. You never know what they could be going through. They could look the happiest on the outside but feel like they are dying on the inside. They could have experienced something traumatic and you would have no clue. Mental health is a silent killer. Mental health is real. I was drowning and dying on the inside crying for help. It was sad because I could help others and make them feel better but couldn't do that for myself. You ever gave someone a motivational speech and then realize that you need one yourself? I was on the verge of breaking down. I was hurt, and I felt empty. I was great at giving good advice and some people would tell me that I should take my own advice but it wasn't that easy. I was so tired. Tired of feeling like I wasn't good enough for anyone. I was tired of waking up every day and barely surviving. I was tired of waking up and not knowing what my purpose was in life. I was tired of saying I was okay when deep down inside I was drowning in my own tears. I felt so alone in this cold world. I kept praying and pushing through and getting told things will get better but when? How much longer do I have to be in tears? How much longer do I have to pretend I am happy at family functions? I was tired of crying and just wanted to be happy. Why did I have to go through all these horrible things if I didn't even plan to be here in the first place?

Depression was eating me up and started to take over my whole body. I would be so worn out from all the demons and voices and would just sleep to help pass the time. I didn't want to wake up because sleeping was so peaceful and living was like I was fighting a war that I would never win. The nighttime was the worst. That's when all the voices would come back but they would come back even louder! It was impossible for me to sleep. They would tell me things like "Kill yourself nobody loves you", "Your better off dead", "Take those pills", "walk to the river let's talk" then when I get to the river and they would tell me "Drown yourself". I was so scared of these voices because they controlled my happiness, my spirt, and my entire body. I wasn't myself anymore. I would try to numb the pain with alcohol, drugs, and pills. I got drunk once to see how it would make me feel. It made me feel so good. I didn't feel anything. I had no worries; no pain and I was finally at peace. I started off slow but eventually I was drinking every day. I became an acholic and it turned into an addiction. After liquor I got introduce to needles that I would shoot in my arm. I was so high and couldn't feel anything. There were days that I would miss work just to go somewhere and do this. This also became an addiction. It got so bad that I would steal family members money just to get high off needles and pills. People would think I was going to work but I was going to get high. I was doing things that I could never see myself doing. By trying to numb the pain I was setting myself up for failure.

Once the alcohol, drugs, and pills wore off I needed more to feel that same numbness I felt before. We trick ourselves into thinking we're numbing the pain but were just making things worse. We might be numbing the pain for a couple hours or maybe even a day but when we get back to our sober self the pain still remains. It's best to face and deal with the pain head on with God. Months later I tried to drown myself. I would hear voices telling me to go further and that no one would care if I left. That night I knew what I was doing wasn't right but I couldn't stop the voices. I got out the water and sat there and cried alone. I prayed to

God and let him know that I needed him. I asked Him to save me. The next day the voices became worse. I called my grandma Karin and told her everything. I told her that I had been molested, I told her how I felt about my father and I poured it all out to her. Little did she know I wasn't calling for help I was calling to tell her what was going on with me, that I loved her, and to say my goodbyes to her. She talked me into not leaving and I can say that was one of the best decisions I ever made. She told me if God can help her beat cancer then He can help me beat depression too. She told me I was braver than I thought I was. She reminded me that I would inspire so many people and to keep going. She believed I had higher gift and purpose in life. This is when she explained to me the difference between regular pain and pain with a purpose. I had pain with a purpose and told me not to give up now. I was the author of my story.

This is when I started my long and steady journey to get better mentally. I know it's hard and I know you feel like the storm may never leave but trust me it's get better. The storm can't and won't last forever just because it's raining now doesn't mean it's going to be raining forever. The rain helps the grass get greener and grow. That is what the rain is doing to you making you stronger and helping you grow in ways you never saw yourself growing. I can promise you that the storm doesn't last forever. I want you to know that it's only over when you choose for it to be over.

A lot of people may have given up on you but don't give up on yourself. God is still rooting for you. All the bad things had to happen in your life in order for all the right things to come together. My highs didn't make me who I am, being at rock bottom did. Don't let depression trick you into taking your life. Let this struggle build you up like my struggle did for me. Let what you been through be a part of your story not the last the chapter of it. That ugly depression chapter you are in right now is going to be one of the most powerful parts of your testimony. Your next chapter will be everything you ever wished for. God is shifting your entire life to be happy, healed, blessed, and to have a better life. If God would've gave us everything we asked for right away we wouldn't appreciate it and value it as much because it wasn't earned. Since you had to go through hell and back just to receive everything, you will value it so much more than just getting it handed to you. Trust God in the storm even if you can't see His process.

Depression isn't like
any other illness
don't be ashamed
you don't have to hide it.

Chapter 9

BROKEN CRAYONS
STILL COLOR

If a crayon breaks it still has value because it can still color. This is the same for us. No matter how broken we may be, no matter how hard things may seem, no matter how many doors have closed, no matter how many people have disappointed you, and no matter how hard things may get, you still are valuable . Many times, we face those same situations and think it's the end of the world. We doubt our self-worth and lose confidence in ourselves to be able to do the things we enjoy doing. You have to keep coloring despite how broken the crayon may be. Keep moving forward with purpose. Instead of letting my brokenness fuel me I let it stop me and drain me. I was an empty car with a dead battery inside. I thought that being heartbroken, fatherless, sexually abused, and depressed, would keep me from living my best life. I wanted everything in my life to be perfect including myself that any setback would cause me to break down, cry and doubt myself.

I would be so hard on myself to the point if one thing went wrong, I would think I was a failure. Sometimes we put too much pressure on ourselves without even realizing it. This can cause you to be mentally and physically drained. I stopped being so hard on myself and started to focus only on the things I could control. For the things that were out of my control I prayed about them and gave them all to God. You can do this by creating a list of all the things you can control such as your positive attitude and positive thought. Then you will create a list for the things that's out of your control from your past and leave those things in God hands. This will help you feel less stressful and more at peace with yourself. I am a walking testimony that God can turn our darkest moments and memories into a beautiful bright light that can lead us to many different paths and inspire many others like you. Nothing that you have been through can stop you from reaching for the stars. Remember that the sky is the limit. . Those things that caused you pain, hurt, and hard times is what shaped you into who you are. If we had to choose one thing to define us it wouldn't be possible because we're a combination of a lot of things that helped us become the growing person we are today. I want you to sit and think where would your life be in a couple years if you didn't give up? Then look back a couple years ago did you think you'll be where you are now? See for me, I didn't think I'd make it this far and survive everything that was sent to destroy me. I never imagined the heartbreaks, the long dark nights balled up with tears, and the nights begging and praying to God for a sign and a way out this cage I was in. I wouldn't trade any of those things I been through because it gave me the strength I needed. It allowed me the opportunity to give others strength and inspire people like you. If I can get through these things so, so can you.

Each and every life event shaped me into the Robert Lawson I am today. I questioned God all my life. I had no clue what I was called to do on this earth but he knew. "For I know the plans I have for you," declares the Lord, "Plans to prosper you and not to harm you, plans to give you hope and a future." (Jeremiah 29:11)

TRIAL AND ERROR

In this verse he tells us that he has plans for us despite all the hardships we might face along the way. You and I are similar to where things have been made to break us but despite every single thing we have been through or how broken we may end up; we won't let that tear us apart. Nothing you went through can stop you from what God called you to do on this earth. You have to be courageous and trust the process. Each day is a chance to make a fresh start. Just because we may have gone through rough situations, doesn't mean we can't operate or provide to the world or ourselves. You can still be broken and beautiful and you can still be broken and accomplish all your dreams and aspirations.

Just because a crayon breaks both parts still works and color the same. It can still give you the same beautiful picture you wanted and desire. Crayons go through a lot of pressure and transformation just like us and still transform into beautiful artwork. A lot of people use those broken crayons to make lip gloss, make up and other beautiful things. That's the same thing with our life we can use those same broken crayons and create a beautiful masterpiece. I never looked at it this way though, I always thought how my ugly brokenness

76

could be used for greatness and to inspire many others like you. I thought my life was a big mess. I didn't think God was even listening to me for trying to take my life so many times. Every time it felt like I was moving ten steps forward it felt like something knocked me a million steps back. I didn't feel like I was good for my brokenness to be turn into a beautiful picture. I didn't feel like I had too much to offer in this world or to God. By feeling like this I didn't even think I had what it took to live up to God's expectations to live through my purpose. I didn't take God's word seriously. I didn't want to be bothered. I pushed everyone away and just wanted to be alone. I needed help, I needed encouragement and I was tired of feeling like this.

Have you ever gone to church and felt like the pastor was talking directly to you? I went to church once and I felt like he was talking directly to me. "He talked about not letting abusers win and go after the life we deserve. Pain is only temporary but if we let it stop us that pain will last a lifetime. He then said a verse from the bible that will always stick with me Revelation 21:4 "He will wipe every tear from their eyes, and there will be no more death or sorrow or crying or pain". That verse stuck with me because it let me know that God will wipe all my tears and my pain away. That means He was listening to me this whole time even though I thought He wasn't. After church I went home and prayed to God in so many different ways while crying. I asked God how could I use my brokenness and turn it into my power. God responded by saying, "You can still use broken crayons can you?" Even though I said yeah, I just didn't know what the heck broken crayons had to do with anything I asked Him. He told me "I healed your grandmother in ways you'll never know and I can do the same for you son". It wasn't until years later where I went out to eat and I saw a little girl crying because her crayon broke and the mom said "It still works baby. See, look." The little girl smiled and continued to color her beautiful picture. "I GOT IT!" I screamed, as the whole restaurant was looking at me like I was crazy.

It's crazy how God will show us so many signs in life but it's up to us to catch those signs. God was basically telling me that I was still broken but he could still use me. I used to ask myself why I had to go through all this pain and lessons in life and I know you probably had the same questions. I may not know all the answers but, I do know God will not leave you or forsake you. You don't understand now because the devil and enemy tricked you and took the truth from you., He will always be there even if you are broken and feel like you can't be repaired. God is the true healer. The scars on your body and heart will become blessings to others that went through the same thing as you. One day you will be amazed about what a beautiful masterpiece you turned into and all the great things God did while you weren't looking.

There is so much greatness and beauty within you so please do not lose faith. Your brokenness will be someone else's blessing and you don't even know it. You might think it doesn't have purpose but to someone else it does. Sometimes it's just part of the process that we all have to go through. I know I will always trust God because he pulled me out some dark places when I didn't even think I could be saved. I am here to tell you that being broken is okay and being broken is still gorgeous. Each day we wake up is chance to start again and make a beautiful start. Just because we may be broken, we still have things to offer. Just like the crayon we can still add value to the paper and continue on our path and purpose in life.

TRIAL AND ERROR

Your life isn't over your life has just begun. A lot of times in life when we look at our disappointments, failures, and remorse, we realize that this is what God uses to make our life so much better. We are God's paper and he is the artist. If he can turn my mess into beauty, then he can do the same thing for you if you allow him to.

Chapter 10

HEALING

---

*Your healing is on the other side of all your
past hurt so keep going; it gets better.*

—Robert Lawson

Healing is one of the first steps to becoming whole
again. We end up becoming someone better, stronger,
and wiser. Being able to confront your pain, past, and
everything you have been through can make you
relentless. Being able to control everything you have
been through can take you to another level. The level

of ultimate happiness and peace. The road to success and the road to healing is always under construction.

As you are moving through life to reach your goals, there are many obstacles and potholes along the road we have to face. This can cause us to be frustrated, uncomfortable, and inpatient. It can be frustrating because we thought maybe the road would be smooth and easy but little do we know that the road was never set up to be smooth. This applies with the healing journey as well. Healing takes you to a different place. Some roads you have to take alone with no significant other, friends, parents, or family. It has to be you and God. You just have to subtract some people out to fix and heal the broken person inside of you. It's not about anyone else when it comes to healing but you. You have to give yourself all the attention you desire before giving it to another person. Take that time to get to know yourself on a more deeper level hand and hand with God. This will help you give yourself the right amount of time to heal to push further into your ultimate goal of being whole, at peace, and achieving happiness.

Your journey never ends. It only begins with your next step so let your next move be your best move. Healing takes you to a place of being separated but that separation will start to feel lonely. You start to find yourself doing life by yourself. The people you talk to a lot tend to become distant. When you are trying to evaluate your life, it causes you to have some level of separation. Evaluation is when you peel off the old pieces of yourself so you can create yourself into a beautiful masterpiece that you always dreamt of being. Don't give up during your healing process as it can be hideous but it will be worth it. The majority of you reading this book have been hurt, damaged, and broken at some point. The same majority including myself are guilty of just sweeping that same hurt under the rug and finding ways to avoid it and move past it. It's time we stop being ashamed of our hurt and of our stories and share them. Half of the people you see every day are going through the same situation as you. They just hide it with fake smiles and snapchat filters.

Cut out the distractions, limit social media, plan, and stick to it. That is the purpose of this book, is to share my story and to inspire someone like you. If I can get through this so can you. You're strong just like me and maybe even stronger. It took me twenty-five years of sleepless nights with tears running down my face, and lots of praying, to allow me to get closer to God. During this time I held on to my faith and did a lot of soul searching. This allowed me to tell my story without crying, and without getting sad. Now when I tell my story I cry tears of joy. Even in writing this book there are many moments where I cried thanking God for healing me and helping me get through everything that was sent to kill me. All my life I was scared and ashamed to tell my story. I let all this hurt and pain hinder my growth, happiness, and peace but I decided that I wouldn't allow this for myself any longer. Our story matters and it's time for us to stop hiding behind it. I used to have everyone fooled that I was so healed including myself. I used to have everyone thinking that I was happy, that my father's absence didn't bother me, and that my heartbreak didn't bother me. Nobody knew about me being sexually abused, only my therapists knew. I was lying to everyone and holding everything in. It wasn't easy confronting everything.

If a person doesn't heal all the way before getting into a new relationship, they will leave a trail of tears and broken hearts everywhere they go. That is what I ended up doing. I was out there hurting people because I was hurt. I met a nice girl by the name of Kendra who didn't mean me no harm. We were together for some months and I ended up doing her wrong. I told her I wasn't going to hurt her and I ended up hurting her the same way Mira did me. What made it worse, is I kept doing her wrong and leading her on because I didn't want to lose her. I wanted the best of both worlds while still trying to find myself. I was truly sorry and I regret hurting her because she didn't deserve that. They say that hurt people hurt people and I was beyond hurt. You can't heal by going from relationship to just to prove to someone that they can be replaced. You might be replacing them but you're not replacing the hurt. You end up adding more hurt to the fire. It's okay to be alone, it's okay to love yourself first. You don't need anyone to love you just so you can feel validated.

A lot of relationships fail because we're so broken but still trying to date as if we are not. Stop trying to prove people wrong. You are wrong. Take accountability for your actions. It's not about them it's about you. You have to do this for you not them. The best revenge is being able to make yourself happy and being able to love yourself in ways nobody else can. Have patience with yourself. Nobody heals overnight. You will get where you need to be in time. For now, just relax and remember every day you heal is a step in the right direction. You have made it through many bad days that you thought you wouldn't make it through. So, keep going and be patient, and be proud of how far you have come. If you are healing don't stop and don't get off the path you are on. Don't let others discourage you or make you seem like you are selfish. The greatest thing you can do is to make yourself feel whole again and that's the best feeling ever. You can't be whole by throwing broken pieces of yourself into the world. You'll eventually have it all figured out. Everything will soon make perfect sense. Believe in yourself, trust yourself, and believe and trust in God. Forget what others think and trust the healing process. Stop asking yourself why, you don't need to know all the answers. Stop questioning everything that comes your way and be ready to execute. You have to be willing to take a seat with your pain and listen to the sadness within your body. Acknowledge your scars and be willing to accept it. Release everything. Let it go and give it to God.

HEALING

The quicker you stop questioning things and trying to figure everything out the sooner you will start healing. Healing is done in the present not the past. Even though it hasn't been easy for me, I am so much closer to where I want to be. Sometimes the biggest part of healing is being honest with ourselves and figuring out that we play a huge part in our own suffering. I was playing a big part of my own suffering by not confronting my pain and lying to myself. How do you expect the pain to stop when you can't even admit you are hurting in the first place? That was me, I was making things worse. Sometimes it's tough to say we need help because we think we have it all figured out. We lie to ourselves and tell ourselves that we are feeling good and that everything is okay.

We feel like we are moving on, but in reality, we are tricking ourselves to avoid the pain. We can all agree it's so much easier to avoid the people and situations that caused us pain. When we suppress our feelings we trick ourselves into thinking we are actually healed. Then something triggers us and now we are faced with emotional and trauma setbacks that were supposed to have already been resolved. It takes a world of courage to admit you need help. I never said it would be easy but it's worth it and you deserve to finally be happy again. You haven't even met the best version of yourself which encompasses finally being healed, being content, and the most satisfied person ever. Meeting this part of you is worth fighting for so keep doing the internal work and get better. You will never be able to move past anything in life until you deal with it. You cannot grow as a person in pain, and in bitterness but, you can use that to push you forward. Forgive yourself so you can transform into something beautiful. Being able to acknowledge the hurt and pain is the first step to getting back to yourself. It's not your fault for all the pain that you have been through and for the pain people caused you. Even though it's not your fault, it is your responsibility to heal from that pain and trauma. You can't expect to heal by staying in the same environment you got hurt in. Some of you are waiting for on an apology to heal your heart, some of you are waiting for someone to save you, some of you are waiting for the right time. I'm going to be real with you. That apology you are waiting for may never come and you might end up waiting forever. You will be waiting forever if you wait on someone else, you have to be willing to want to save yourself.

Lastly, there will never be a right time. There will always be an obstacle or setback so don't miss out on what you can accomplish by waiting on the right time. Stop giving your heart back to the painful situations and expecting them to change. One day I woke up and the first thought I had was I can't suffer any longer. I told myself I was going to give this healing journey a shot. I was sick of hindering my own growth, and tired of going through the same things. The pain was there and I just had to accept it, heal, and learn from it. I learned I had to believe in myself no matter if no one else believed in me. I decided to see a therapist and join a trauma treatment group. The group had a lot of people like me and it made me feel comfortable with sharing my story. By being a part of the group, I grew out of anger and learned I had to give everything to God. I learned so much about myself and grew so much confidence within myself. I had to do the work on myself in order to love myself better, love my wife better and my three children. If I wasn't healed, I couldn't give myself the life I deserved nor them. I started to feel like I could do this and I never looked back since. I was finally feeling whole again. I was finally able to see the bigger picture of everything I had been through. When I say God is real, God is real.

TRIAL AND ERROR

There were plenty of nights where I thought I would never get out this darkness and he made a way. He was my light when I had no direction. Even when I didn't believe in Him at times, He never stopped believing in me.

I know it may be hard because we always hold on to something that we really want. Just because they damage you doesn't mean they have to be the one to repair you. Just because they broke your heart into a million pieces doesn't mean they have to be the one to fix all those pieces. Just because we hold on to something and really want it in our life that doesn't mean it's good for our soul. There's is no timetable for healing so, its okay if you thought you had it all figure out. It's even okay if you lose control after you thought you had everything under control. You're strong not weak so, don't let the healing process discourage you. It can be messy but also beautiful at the same time. You will get to that happy place again, this time you will understand why everything played out the way it did. It took me a long time to get to that place. I was lost and felt so good to finally be found. It felt good to smile without filters or faking it. It feels good telling my story and not feeling bitter or angry anymore. You will get to that point and when you do praise God because He is so awesome.

Chapter 11

LET GO!

Never go back. Not next week, not next year. The person that treated you wrong will continue to do it the more you accept the lies. The more you go back, the less they value you. They will think you will always be there for them because you always kept running back.

—Robert Lawson

Sometimes we hold on to something because we think that is the best thing to do. We train our hearts and minds that we must stay in that situation because we have to. We put up with things that we shouldn't such as lies, cheating, toxic situations, emotional abuse, narcissist abuse and more. This can cause so much pain, hurt, and can disappoint us a million times and still we find every reason to hold on because we think we have to. We get to a point where we feel bad for trying to finally move and that forces us to hold on even more. We think of how much history we have with this person; how good the bond was and sometimes we just don't want to start over with the next person. I want you to know that someone can come into your life and treat you better in five months than someone did in five years so never settle. What one person takes for granted another person is praying for a chance to treat you right. We hold on because were afraid of what it might look without them in our lives.

Everyone is not meant for your journey. The things we go through and contribute to others makes us a better individual. Everybody isn't meant to be in your life for the long ride. Some are just here to help us grow and teach us lessons that will keep you away from taking bigger losses along the way. Even though we can't control our emotions all the time and things seem to take a toll over our life, try your best to stay focused on the lesson not the person. And most of all be thankful. The lesson is what's going to help you grow when letting go. Don't get so caught up on with what you are letting go of. Focusing on what you are letting go keeps you in a position to where you are only seeing the pain instead of the lesson. Turn that hurt into something powerful. We even hold on for all the wrong reasons. When you come to this point you must ask yourself why? Why do you keep putting yourself into this predicament? Why do you stay when there's someone out there that's better? Why are you a believer of there lies? Why do you keep falling in love with potential? And most importantly why you keep going back if you are not happy? I know you think they're going to change and often times we convince ourselves they are but really, they are not going to. Somewhere deep down in your heart you know they are not going to change. I know the feeling but I'm here to tell you that you been holding on too long and it's time to finally get the strength and let go.

Queen be with the guy that adored you the first time not after you gave him a million chances because the right person you will only need to give one chance to. King be with the lady that loves you for you and pushes you to be great. It's time to get the rest you deserve. You have been so exhausted and drained so take a deep breath and close your eyes. Imagine how much relief you'll have once you finally let go. Now, I want you to never forget that feeling. Commit to it letting go of all those things and people who caused you more harm than good. This pertains to friendships, relationships, situation-ships and even family. Family can be toxic and hurtful too. I always had an issue with holding on to family too. I kept holding on no matter how bruised my heart was. Holding on can sometimes do more damage than letting go. I was scared to let go because of my abandonment issues. I was trying to hold on to the one piece that kept me stable at times and I was scared to be alone again. I know it can feel lonely and you want your loved ones to love you through everything like you do for them. To all my Queens and Kings, I want you to remember this, a person that really loves you will not put you through hell just for them to prove you are the one. You should never feel like you have to compete with the next person, make yourself look foolish behind closed doors, or jump a million hurdles just to get their love and attention. Never forget you are the prize; you are the trophy and one of the strongest and bravest around.

LET GO!

All you need is yourself and God. You will make it through I believe in you.

I can give you all the tips and all the hints of letting go but until you believe in yourself or find something that works for you, you'll forever be stuck holding on. When someone is not right for you and we don't listen to the signs God sends, He will allow that person to continue to hurt you until you have no choice but to let go. I know it may sound harsh but it is so true. God gives us warnings. Those same warnings are warnings before destruction. We have to stop being in denial and learn how to walk away and let go. When we ignore God's signs, we think He is punishing us but we are really punishing ourselves. Don't put your key to happiness in someone else's hands. We tend to build our homes in others. We invest in this home and decorate it with all fancy things. Then we base our self-worth by how these same people treat and value us in that home. We get excited because everything seems so perfect. This makes us forget that when investing and building your home inside of someone else we give them the privilege to make us feel less of a person. They have the power to make us go back to square one with our living conditions. Hold on to your own keys and make yourself happy.

When a person hurts you whether its friends, family, or an ex and you have a hard time letting go, you are still giving them the chance to hurt you even deeper. I know it hurts and you may even want revenge but the best revenge is to let it go, get your life together, and let them watch what a blessing you are inside and out. God saw how they hurt you, He saw how many nights you cried, He saw you ready to give up, He saw everything. God said if you let go of everything, He will give you back everything that you lost and restore it with something so much better. That promotion you have always been waiting for, the new job, house, car, beautiful relationship etc. God will replace it all. Letting go doesn't mean it's the end it means it's the start of something better. You hold the power to your happiness don't let someone else get the power to control whether you are happy or sad. We have to also let go of blame. Blaming yourself, other people and blaming God doesn't get us anywhere. Blaming isn't going to change anything so let it go! Letting go is being able to find peace, forgiveness, and being able to accept everything. No, I'm not saying it was okay for what they did but I'm saying it happened and at some point, we have to get the courage to let it go and move on like they did. It will get better sooner or later so trust the process. You don't deserve to be taken advantage of or broken into a million pieces. Don't be afraid to start over you might like this new start better. Sometimes letting go isn't always about relationships or other things. Letting go can also mean letting go of doubt, fear, self-doubt, and other things. The past is the past and no matter how hard we try to change it we just won't.

You have to let go of the past but keep all the lessons it taught you. What's destined for you will come knocking at your door. You have to change your focus and focus on your goals, glow up, and grind harder. Stop checking up on them and let them go and check up on yourself. It all starts and end with you not them.

Chapter 12

FORGIVENESS

It took me years to understand what forgiveness was all about. I always thought how could I forgive someone that hurt me, destroyed me, and made me a second option. I always thought how I could forgive my dad for abandoning me, not being there for me, and causing so much pain and trauma within his own seed? After doing a lot of research I realize forgiveness isn't about accepting the bad things they did to you it's about letting it all go and preventing it from doing more damage to your heart. Forgiveness isn't for the person that caused your life damage it's for you. Its saying "You're not that important to control my life". Its saying "I'm taking back control of my own life". You are worthy of a bright future, peace, and happiness. I always felt that I couldn't forgive the people who hurt me no matter how hard I tried. Then God came into my room one day and told me "How can I forgive you for you sins if you can't forgive them for there's". That's when I decided to try this forgiveness thing.

Forgiveness doesn't mean to rekindle things. Leave them behind and go after the life you deserve. Forgiveness doesn't mean I have to give you a chance back into my life like before. It means I don't hold any bitterness or hurt feelings against you. It means I'm getting myself together from the hurt that I caused and allowed along the way. Pay attention to the thing's life shows you. Sometimes you'll be given the same lessons just in different ways to see if you learned anything. You can forgive someone and not ever have to talk to them again. You don't always have to seek closure, the only person that can give you closure is you. The very first step in forgiveness is forgiving yourself and accepting what was done to you. That's something I didn't do. I blamed myself for my father leaving and not wanting to be in my life and I blamed myself for Mira leaving as well. Forgive yourself before you forgive anyone. Don't become a prisoner to your past by always reliving your mistakes or what if scenarios. You cannot forgive anyone if you are not willing to forgive yourself first. This is something that's a must if you ever want to move on. It can be very easy to put everything on ourselves You then start to hate yourself, feel different about yourself, and you start thinking you were wrong. The thing is you weren't wrong all along. The people that hurt you were. You were absolutely right to trust, love, and give chances. Don't you hate yourself because they were evil and hurt you. Just because you are forgiving them doesn't mean you have to call or text to forgive them. You forgive them in your hearts.

I was able to forgive my father after years of pain and suffering. We went out to eat and I let him meet my son the only child I had at the time. I wanted to give my son the chance to meet his grandfather. It wasn't about me anymore it was about him and their bond. Everything was so perfect and it's a memory I will never forget I have all the pictures they took together and that memory will always remain priceless in my mind. My father and I would talk more often and our bond grew. Just when I thought things couldn't get any better, they got worst. I wanted to ask my father an honest question. The question was how come you were never really there? How come we weren't close how we should've been? All he kept doing was beating around the bush and blaming everything on my mother. My mother didn't make him sell drugs; my mother didn't make him live the life that he lived. He picked that life on his own. My mother didn't tell him to get locked up and be in and out of prison. He made those choices on his own. I got upset because all I was looking for was the truth, that's it. He would say little slick stuff like about my son's name. I never understood how he could make comments about his grandson. He texted me one day to see if he can borrow fifteen dollars and we ended up arguing. After we argued back and forth I told him I forgive him but I will never let another man raise my kids or do them how he did me. Even though I wasn't trying to hurt him with my response I was just expressing to him the truth. He hurt me with his response. He said, "You're not my son anyway, that's why you tried to kill yourself over that girl" and that just shot me down so bad. All I could do is block the messages because I was so hurt. Months later I unblocked him and he ended up calling couple days later. I didn't want to deal with him so I responded. "I love you but I don't mess with you like that. I'm sorry I have to love myself man". He told me "I was just calling you and telling you the same" which I felt was a lie. I told him he needed to grow up . He told me "I will kill you and when I see you it's on sight." He also said, "I will have your little sister knock you out". What father tells their own son that they will kill them? I never will understand.

Yes, I forgave him with everything in me but as a father with three children I just couldn't understand. I love my children and I will never hurt them how my father hurt me. Sometimes you just have to love family from a distance no matter how much you love and care for them. When you stop seeing certain people as cousin, mom, dad, aunt, and uncles and start looking at them as spirit for spirit then your life will be so much better. You have to stop letting family do you wrong just because you were brought up on "Family is everything" or "Family over everything". Family can sometimes bring bad spirits in your life and when that happens you have to readjust yourself and remove those bad spirits out of your life. I had to forgive my father because I was holding up my own life. It wasn't about him anymore it was about me. The longer you hold on to the anger and the pain the more you will be stuck living in it. It's time for a cleanse with your mind, body, spirit and people. Prayer really works. I couldn't hang on to the hurt and the bitterness. I had to learn how to forgive. Yes, it was hard but you have to do it for you. I had to also do it for my children. I prayed and got on my knees and asked God to cleanse me inside and out and remove all this anger from my mind, body and spirit. A couple months later I started to feel calm, happy, and at peace. I couldn't be happier with the person I became and I am finally at a point where I'm happy. I forgave everyone in my past who has caused me pain and hurt. The majority of the people I forgave have never apologized for the things they did to me. Which is fine. I had to forgive them because my healing was more vital to me than holding hatred towards them. I wanted to do what was possible to not cause more suffering on my end. I had to forgive and start loving myself. So, forgive and start loving yourself.

Chapter 13

KNOW YOUR WORTH

You're worth so much more than what you settle for. I want you to stop selling yourself short. I see women always talking about how they want a good man but they always keep running back to the man that's no good. I see men who say they want a good woman but mess up what they have for something so temporary. I also have seen guys with a woman who is no good for them but settle. You have to believe that you are worth more and stop settling for anything. If you don't stand for something you will fall for anything. If you don't stand for your self-worth and your value you will be misled by anything coming your way. If you don't appreciate your self-worth and value yourself why would someone else? Don't think someone is supposed to love you or respect you if you don't love yourself. Respect yourself enough to cut ties with anyone who doesn't respect, value or make you happy. Put yourself first for a chance. You have been second your whole life from others and from yourself. You have to think how you would want your life to be and never stop chasing that life. We have to stop chasing everything that give us no worth or value.

You have been pouring into everyone else focusing on everyone else so it's time to pour into you and focus on yourself. It's time to evaluate your life and bloom so when you look back you can see how much you have grown in life. How many times have you caught yourself getting mad about how bad they treated you? Next, I want you ask yourself why are you still there with them? You might say because they are great in bed, they have money, they buy you nice things, etc. Let me tell you this, you are worth more than sex and money. If they are not trying to get to know you and connect with you on a deeper level, they're not the one for you. Just because they give you great sex and buy you nice things and have money, it doesn't give them the opportunity to call you out your name, manipulate you, make you feel lesser of who you are. What I'm trying to say is that if they don't know your worth you have the power to know your worth and leave any situation that's not aligning with you. You have to stop dumbing down to their lies and stop letting them break into your happiness. Never let someone get too comfortable with treating you wrong. Love yourself first.

There are tons of people out there who would love you the correct way. You will find someone that will help you build an empire, that will treat you like the queen or king you are and will give you the attention you deserve. Don't settle for just anything. Find someone that really loves you and shows it every day not just on a holiday. I always knew I was worth so much, but I kept treating myself like I was a penny when I worth more than that. I would always come up short like a 4th and 1 football conversion. I would date girls just to think I needed to feel loved. They would use me and tell other females, "Girl, go talk to Robert he will buy you anything," as they would say. They would tell their friends I'm sweet and to use me. Being used started to become a thing I became used to. I thought they were coming to me because they liked me and wanted to get to know me but they were just trying to use me to do things for them. They would even tell people, "Girl talk to Robert he offered to buy my baby some pampers and shoes, I don't even like him for real I'm just using him". I Started to feel like girls didn't even want a good man for real. I say that because when they get one, they are not used to it and take advantage of them or do them wrong.

Women always choose to love the bad guy over a nice guy because they want something fun to chase. Women always ask for a better man but they love to be loved by a person that's not good for them. I see some women post that they don't want a sensitive man and want someone that's going to put them in their place when they argue. That just shows they want someone different. My last relationship and the people that used me taught me so much about myself. They taught me how to value myself and not let someone dictate my value because they will put an outdated sticker on you. They taught me to never beg someone else for love and attention. I always thought I needed to feel loved, be in a relationship to be happy, and needed someone to love me to be alright. Truth is I only needed to love myself because self-love is the best love. You know yourself better than anyone else so nobody can love you better than you. I used to beg for girls to talk to me and to get their attention I used pay girls to date me. I was so silly for love I would do anything to finally feel accepted. I forgot that I was the prize too. I forgot who I was and that I am worth way more than I was choosing to settle for. They taught me how to not lower my standards and that your standards are never too high for the right one. It taught me don't chase after nobody that doesn't want to be chased and not to keep someone who doesn't want to be kept. Never waste your time and love on someone who don't deserve or want it. Sometimes we even try and pray about things and wonder why they didn't get answered. Sometimes they are not answered because you are worth way more than what you are asking God for. We have a big God so we have to stop speaking so small. No dream or anything is too big for him to fulfill. Get out of your comfort zone and get out of that box you are in. Get to know yourself, the real you. Love yourself, be there for yourself. This will help attract the right people.

You're a blessing so act like one. Sometimes being weak has nothing to do with leaving something behind but it can show you how mentally strong you can be. We finally walk away not because we got them to realize our worth but we finally got the opportunity to realize it. You know you have a lot to offer and bring more than enough to the table so it's okay to stand alone. We also think to ourselves that losing the person you love is the most painful thing ever. Once you know your worth people will be so mad because they don't have access to you like they once did. Once you know your worth life becomes so much easier. We lose ourselves to someone who doesn't deserve us. The best thing is when you get your self-worth back, and when you have the strength to walk away. You feel like you can breathe again. Be there for yourself how you want everyone else to be there for you. You're your best friend so pat yourself on the back, encourage yourself and be patient with yourself. Take yourself on dates, self-care days, mental health days, buy yourself gifts, shoes, flowers, sports games it all starts with you. You don't need anyone to do these things for you. Yeah, it might feel good for someone to do it but it'll always feel better when you can do it for yourself. You have to make sure you are staying true to your word because nobody will be there for you like you. Go out with your friends, rest, celebrate your wins and don't let anyone minimize what you accomplished already because you deserve it. Love the person you are becoming just like you wanted everyone else to love you.

I got tired of being treated like I was the floor and everyone is just walking past stepping on me every day. I know how it feels to be treated poorly, I know how it feels to text a person multiple times, begging to be treated the correct way and giving them a million chances. The more time I got to know myself and spend by myself the more I realized it don't take all of that pain for someone to love you. If someone really love you, they wouldn't put themselves in a situation where they are going to lose or jeopardize the relationship. If someone really love you, they wouldn't put you in situation where you have to act out of character or argue with the next guy or girl. Learn your worth and put yourself first. I got up and left every person that disrespected my worth. When you are tired you are tired and I reached my breaking point with everyone including myself. I had to change for the better. I had to go out and realize I was worth way more than what I was allowing people to treat me. If you allow people to treat you any kind of way, they will continue to think that it's okay. I wasn't having it anymore everyone thought I was acting funny but I just finally realized I was worth so much more. I will always strive to teach my daughter and my two boys to know their worth because there were many times, I didn't know mine. Now that I know my worth, I will never settle for anything less than that ever again. Not a job, not a relationship, friendship, family member you name it. Never stop striving to know your worth. Until you know your worth you will always be stuck settling for anything.

Chapter 14

GRIEF

---

*Death feels like losing a
person over and over again.*

—Robert Lawson

I never thought I would go through something like
that. Growing up I never believed in death because I
never really had someone close to me pass away. My
auntie Monday would always say "we going to die and
come back a different race and color." So, if God
created you black you might be white or Mexican next
time. Crazy huh? Yeah, I know. I believed it and I was

never scared of death. It wasn't until February 27, 2021, that I received a call from my mother's husband at 8am. He said, "you need to get over here your grandma passed away." My heart dropped; I couldn't believe it. I got there and all I could do is cry and wish it wasn't true. Like I said earlier my grandma had been battling cancer for a while. She beat it once and it just kept coming back on and off. She used to also go to chemotherapy. She was a true fighter and a warrior. The rock and glue of our family. I miss and love her so much. I never knew grief would be this hard and everyday I'm still learning how to grieve in healthy ways.

Just when you think you got this life stuff figured out something like death hits your life. It is a learning process so never stop learning. She was always so happy and proud of the man I was becoming. She would always praise me for being a family man, good father, and just being me. She would always tell me I remind her of her and how I always cared for others. I remember one day at school I had a spelling test and I got an A+ and I came home so excited to tell her. She would always tell me "Robbie you have brain power" and "you're going to be something so great one day even you're not going to believe it." Those two things will always be with me even when the devil will trick me into thinking to give up and end my life. I would tell myself I have brain power; you will not get to me this time. My grandma has a huge impact on my life and many others as well. Two weeks before she passed, she told me I had a higher gift and purpose in life. I never knew what she meant so I asked her and she said I cannot tell you. She told me I would have to figure it out on my own. So, after she passed, I kept seeing the same signs coming through my phone on social media about depression, being fatherless, and other things I had previously went through. All my life I had been missing God's signs and I just couldn't miss them this time.

I believe my purpose is to tell my story and impact the world in so many ways. I thank my grandma every day for leading me to my calling and purpose. Just when you think God forgot about you, He will lead you right to where you need to be. It might not be the way you would like it to be but it's the way he knows is best. Grieving can vary from person to person. I'm not here to tell you it's going to be easy. Deep down inside it'll never be okay, we just learn how to deal with it.

TRIAL AND ERROR

Nothing in life prepares you for this moment. One minute you might be fine and next you just start thinking about them and tears fall down your face. Some days you get mad at the world and don't want to talk to anyone but then again you really want someone you can talk to about this. Sometimes you wish you can have just one more hug, kiss, and talk. Then other times you start crying even more because you'll never get a chance to get those things. One minute you're bawling your eyes out and the next minute you can't even cry no matter how hard you try. Trying to accept the fact you're never going to see someone that help raised you or shared memories with can be so hard. I hated that God took my grandma away but my grandma was always in pain and always suffering due to her cancer. She might've made it look easy but I had to stop being selfish and look at the bigger picture. When she passed, she just laid there so peaceful and finally getting the rest she deserved. Yeah, I wish things could've worked out differently but sometimes we can't control how things work out and death is one of them.

People always say time heals all wounds I'm not here to tell you that. Yes, time does makes things better.

GRIEF

After a while you don't cry like you used to, you'll laugh and smile at times. You might even have some good days but that scar is still there you just learn to wear it well. It's a scar that will never leave. It's like it's a broken bone on cold days it's still going to hurt regardless. Never let anyone tell you it's time to move on. Take your time and grieve as long as you think you need too. Grieving is a long and hard process. Some days you don't know if you're coming or going. Social gatherings, interactions, conversations are sometimes hard because you really just want to break down out of nowhere. If you see people posting on social media but they stop texting you, stop being offended. It honestly is sometimes easier to cope by posting than actually talking. If people don't understand it or don't want to communicate with you the way you need to through your process, that's fine. If you love someone enough, you'll do whatever to help them through it. Be there for them but don't make their process harder. There will never be a day I don't think about my grandma. I will forever do right and do all the right things she would have wanted me to do. I Thank her for giving me so much to live for and for that I'll forever be grateful.

Chapter 15

YOUR WHY

Your why has to be bigger and greater than you.

—Robert Lawson

It's so important to have and understand your why in life. There might be days where you don't feel like getting up in the morning, you feel lost, unmotivated, and feel like you can't go any further. This is when your why will push you forward in ways you never thought you could go. When you have that why it pushes you to another level. Your why has to be bigger than yourself. If you are doing it for yourself, you might quit or not give it your all but when you are doing it for someone else you have a greater purpose.

The famous football player and future hall of famer Tom Brady is a great example of having a why. Tom Brady's mom has cancer and has been battling cancer while he was playing football. Tom Brady made it to the super bowl five years ago with the New England Patriots. They were down 28-3 in the third quarter. There was no way they could come back down 25 points with one quarter to go. One of his teammates Julian Edelman kept reminding him that this for his mom. Everyone started playing harder and they came back and won. One of the greatest super bowl comebacks in history. So, what I'm trying to say is your why will fuel you in ways you can't even explain. On those days you don't want to get up for work and you just let the alarm clock ring your why has to be louder than that alarm. So, when you are thinking about your why you have to tell yourself, do I continue to sleep in or do I do it for them. My why is my wife, kids, grandma, and my mom. Everything I do is for my wife and kids. If I'm not bettering myself, they aren't getting better. When your why is great enough you'll always conquer your struggles. I think about my wife and kids every day. I get up every morning and chase my passion, dream, and go out and build relationships with different mentors, and speakers, so I can make the path easier for my children. That's what a father is supposed to do. The reason why you are not living right, oversleeping in the mornings, and laying around is because you are still on 50 percent. You are not giving it your all.

I used to think why the world was passing me by and everyone was living life but I wasn't giving it 100 percent. I said I was but I really wasn't. The reason you are not where you need to be is because you are only thinking about yourself. We can't go back to living paycheck to paycheck. We can't go back to our old living conditions. You have to stop making everything about you. There are people depending on you and people counting on you so get up and make it happen. Greatness is within you so leave your mark every single day. If you want to accomplish your goals and have a successful life you must have a why. I do what I do because I want to give my children everything I never had. I do what I do because I want to give my wife the life she deserves. I do what I do to make my mom proud. I do what I do so my children don't have to go through what I went through. Before my grandma passed, she told me she was going to be on my virtual graduation to see me graduate. She got to see me graduate high school and said she wasn't going to miss my college graduation. She became my why because even though she is not here anymore she's still here within me and it fueled me to graduate college and make her proud. When you are doing it for someone else it makes everything worth it. Be hungry for something beyond you and keep going so you can get more out of life.

There were so many times I wanted to quit and give up but I looked at my wife and kids and my grandma's picture every day and I just kept going. I even look at this post my mom said when I graduated high school, "For the second time in my life I get to witness my baby boy walk across the stage! This time will be much harder, and I'm still not sure how to truly let go. Son, please know there is not a time in your life that you haven't made me proud of you. I've watched you take your first steps and speak your first words. When we didn't have much, I remember on Christmas you are screaming' "mommy look Santa brought me books" Never change the simplicity of your heart! I'm a very tough mom and I know I've drilled an even tougher love but guess what son it paid off! Love has never been easy for me, and as a child I yearned for love. At 17 you came into my life, and it's hard to put into words especially a mother's love, because the depth is unfathomable! You gave me the love I've always wanted. You haven't had the opportunities as many, you yearned for a dad, and was picked on because of your height but you didn't skip a beat and have an amazing heart and personality. You're a model child and my advice to you is to go where there is no paths and leave a trail. Never be afraid to be Robert Lee Lawson, and never follow anyone. You've built the man you are so led by example and always put God first and the future belongs to you as long as you continue to believe in the beauty of your dreams." Little does she know I read this every morning and every night before I go to sleep. This fuels me every day but it just reminds me, I am a model child and I do have a gift and purpose and this is my purpose.

I decided to take her advice and make my own path and lead my own trail and legacy. They are my whys. They are the reason why I keep going when I feel defeated and the reason I keep going when I'm running out of gas. I want to inspire people who were fatherless and went through depression and feel like they can't move forward. I want to break generational curses. My dad told me that his dad wasn't really there and my father wasn't really there for me so I had to be the father to my children and break the generational curses. You have to understand life will hit you with things bigger and harder than yourself, so when you get hit and your why isn't bigger than you, you're going to crumble! Your WHY has to be bigger than you! You'll quit if it's just for you, but if it's something deep down that even if you get knocked down that spirit will never be crushed.

Chapter 16

YOU OWE IT TO YOURSELF

You owe it to yourself to be happy and at peace. Sometimes you can't describe how a person makes you feel, why you stick around so long, and what makes you go all in with them. We can't control those things but we can control how everything plays out though. We can control how we allow them to affect us, and how long we hold on to everything. We have the power to make ourselves happy. We have the power to move forward if things are not going right. We tend forget these things; we forget happiness starts with us. Happiness is a choice. We owe it to ourselves to make us happy. Go after all your dreams, goals, and aspirations. You have to take ownership of your own life.

Life has an expiration date and none of us know when that's going to be so, what will people remember you by? Be something your kids can be proud of, leave a legacy behind. I now make sure I am giving more than 100 percent in life and if not, then I won't do it. We have to stop placing blame on other people and hold ourselves accountable. You must look yourself in the mirror and give yourself an explanation on why you are not living to your full potential. Until you get to that point where you realize you not living up to your full potential you going to forever blame other people. All my life I was blaming my dad for not being in my life and making mistakes and choosing to live like that. We have to stop blaming our parents. We're grown and we make our own. Quit using what you have been through, as a way to be a messed-up person inside and out. Being grown and still blaming your parents, friends and your ex for how you are is something you have to stop. You have to come to a point in life where you stop blaming them and start pointing the finger at yourself. You haven't gotten over it because you don't really want to. That's nobody's fault but your own. I had to stop blaming my father for everything and start pointing the finger at myself. I was the one that didn't want to get over it. I was the one that didn't want to heal.

At some point you have to take accountability for your actions and decide that you want a better outcome for yourself. I had to understand he might not have been there like I wanted him to but he didn't stop me from learning and growing I stopped myself. I had to realize my heartbreak didn't stop me from reaching certain goals, I stopped myself. Most of our parents did what they could with the little that they had. Now it's our turn to go out and look ourselves in the mirror and stop hiding from the truth. You can't blame anyone for the things that did or didn't happen in your life. We have the choice to make things better or worse. Those decisions are up to us not anyone else. The reason we fail or make mistakes isn't someone else's fault, it falls in our own lap. We have to stop blaming our parents for the disaster we create on our own, or our spouses for the reason we're not happy.

Stop blaming the government for the reason you have no money and stop blaming your children because of some of the opportunities you lost along the way. Stop blaming your job and coworker for why you not where you want to be career wise. Michael Jordan was cut from his high school basketball team. Did he blame anyone? No, he pointed the finger at himself and said that's on me, I need to get better and came back the next year and get on the team. He went to the NBA and won not one but six NBA championships. We may be not in control but one hundred percent of the things that come are way are because of how we take them on. How you handle certain situations is based off of the choice you make not anyone else. Pointing the finger at others instead of looking at yourself in the mirror only makes you feel better when you are not supposed to feel that way. It hides the issue when you should be looking for a way to solve it. We have to learn to take full ownership of the way we handle things and be ready to pay the price for what it leads to. You will never become the person you want to be if you keep blaming others for the reasons behind who are you. Ever since I started blaming me for all the messed-up decisions in my life everything has been so much better. If I don't have money, I look for ways to save better. If certain people in my life are not treating me correctly then it's a direct correlation of how I allowed them to treat me that way.

A NOTE FROM THE AUTHOR

Taking ownership and accountability allows you to build character and self-respect. That's what it takes to change everything. Anything that happen in my life is because I let it slide. It's a part of who I am. I woke up one morning and just looked myself in the mirror and stop making excuses and said what are you doing? Blaming them was the easy way out but it didn't change my outcome. So, I had to do a lot of soul searching and it became one of the best decisions I ever made. If you are not where you want to be in life go back and look at the choices you made along the way because it truly helps. I stopped blaming my mother, my father, my friends, cousins, aunts, etc. , Every time something bad happened I stop blaming it on other people. It doesn't matter what the outcome was I started to ask myself what I could have done differently to create a better outcome. I started pointing the finger back at myself and realized no one was going to care for me like I care for myself so I need to be responsible for myself. You have to make a choice that this is going to stop here and no longer let it keep going. It's never too late to turn your decisions around. I had to realize what choices I was going to make for myself now. It didn't have nothing to do with my mother or father and I'm a grown man now so, I had to make some different choices and put myself and my family in a better position. Those choices made me look at life differently. Those choices made me a better person. Even if the people around you are making terrible choices what choices are you going to make? It all starts with you; you have the opportunity to make better choices and live a healthier life and lifestyle. Just because someone treated you wrong you still have the choice to treat yourself right. Just because someone left your life you still have a lot of opportunities to show up for yourself. It doesn't start with them it starts with you. I think the best thing I ever did in life is dig deep within myself and ask myself why I act like this and why I do certain things. It takes a lot of accountability and honesty but getting to know yourself on a more spiritual and deeper level will help you conquer so many things in life.

ABOUT THE AUTHOR

Robert Lawson was born in South Haven MI and raised in a small town called Covert and Coloma MI. He graduated from the University of Phoenix with a bachelor's degree in Healthcare Administration. Robert started off by caring for the elderly and soon found his passion for sharing his story and empowering as many people as he could. Robert's vision is to help people break loose from childhood trauma and to learn how to heal. He believes you can use that pain as your power instead of letting the pain use you. The passing of his grandmother Karin Taylor allowed him to find out his true calling in life and that is what led him to start writing his own books. He was featured on the Real Deal Podcast. Robert enjoys playing basketball, football, reading books and was awarded National Honor Society of Leadership and Success (Sigma Alpha Pi) by University of Phoenix. Robert is available for book signings and author features.

A NOTE FROM THE AUTHOR

Thank you for taking the time out to read through my journey with me. I hope what you have read has allowed you to take full responsibility of your life, inspired you in more ways than before. This book has come to an ending, but your journey to creating the life you want and desire is a never-ending process. In life when you really want something do you go after it or do you just wait for someone to give it to you? If you answer, go after it you are correct! Going after what you desire indicates that you are the right person for it. Claiming your position in life is a journey about you and the way you associate with the world and the things near you. If you don't go after the life you deserve you are giving others the opportunity to give you a life you don't deserve. Instead of you shaping your life and life experiences they will do it for you. The world itself, social media, music, and other things will start to have a toll on you if you haven't figured out your responsibilities in your life. If your mind is impacted easily in a bad way then it'll forever be hard for you to get where you need to be in life. You cannot go out and face the world if you don't have the right mindset. That is my purpose and my goal is to help you develop the right tools within you so you can conquer the world like you are destined to. We must knock down our family old cycle. We can start by going out and ripping up all the negative plants that our families planted. Then replant them with better things. To everyone reading this if you want to travel down a different road, you must get rid of the old path. Get rid of everything that try to stop you from reaching for the stars. If your family has a history of bad habitats, it's up to you to put a stop to it. To not make the same mistakes our families made we must know what they did wrong and the history behind it. We must learn what held back our mothers, fathers, and other family members and use that understanding to make better choices which will lead us to a better life. When you know better you will do better in life and sometimes that's all it takes. That's all it took for me. If our families want us to live a certain way, it's easier for us to take they route. It takes a special someone like you with a lot of courage to travel where there is no path laid out for you with faith to create your own path. Step out on faith street and leave the cycle your family created. I declare you to make better choices for your future. I was always taught: the goal was to be better than our mother and father but I was always taught wrong. The goal is to be better for us so, be better for you.

BIBLIOGRAPHY

The extent of fatherlessness. National Center for Fathering. (2022, October 12). Retrieved October 13, 2022, from https://fathers.com/statistics-and-research/the-extent-of-fatherlessness/

World Health Organization. (2021, September 13). *Depression*. World Health Organization. Retrieved January 13, 2023, from https://www.who.int/news-room/fact-sheets/detail/depression

Made in the USA
Coppell, TX
26 February 2023

13449259R00085